Angels
Never Lie

Angels
Never Lie

Everyday Miracles, Angelic Encounters
and Lives Transformed by Love

Gerald A. Van Slyke

revised edition---new ISBN will be 0-9785689-0-7

10 9 8 7 6 5 4 3 2 1

For information, address:
    Lord and Daniels Publishing, Inc.
    7705 E. Sheridan St.
    Scottsdale, AZ 85257-1634
    Email: LordandDanielsPublishingInc@yahoo.com
    Telephone: (480) 545-0570

Edited by Pamela A Van Slyke and Patricia Spadaro
Cover art: "Angel Sunset" by Kevin Charles Miller, www.Kevinsheaven.org
Cover design by Manjari Graphics, www.manjarigraphics.com

To those brave souls who are unafraid of speaking the truth of their encounters with angels, Spirit, and loved ones who have passed on.

To Gregory Van Slyke, Rachael, John Peters, Susan and Ariel.

And to Miles and Marlie: Here's a toast to you, wherever you two are and whatever you're doing. Ya did good.

Contents

Stories

Acknowledgments

I am especially grateful to Pamela, the mother of our three children, for believing in me and for her encouragement and continued prodding to keep me focused to see this project through to the end.

A bowlful of gratitude and thanks also goes to all those involved with putting these pages between the covers and their hard work and patience with me to get the job done.

I thank those who entered my life along the way and who unknowingly lent light and encouragement along my writing path: Dr. Wayne Dyer, Dannion Brinkley, Doreen Virtue, Nick Bunick, Julia Ingram, and the Mishka Production founders, Ariel Wolfe and Liz Dawn.

A special thanks goes to William Chiles (Pila of Hawaii) for his friendship as this book was being written and his constructive criticism, humor, professionalism and jokes that helped keep me grounded and stay the course. Semper fidelis and welcome home. Mahalo nui lao and aloha, my friend. Cock-a-doodle-doo.

To all those close to me who never wavered (you know who you are), thank you. To Alicia, Curtis and Bradley, my children, a gift from the One and All: you never cease to give me joy, countless smiles, and unconditional love. My love back to you, twice.

Spiritual thanks and profound gratitude for the support of the angels who guided and inspired me every step of the way in writing this book. I couldn't have done it without them. Before writing a letter on a page or even touching the keyboard, I asked for divine intervention. Meditation and prayers always came first, the writing second. I started out with a rough outline, but I'll be damned if I know where I put it. I asked for guidance and it was received. For that I am forever grateful.

To Pixie, the Brittany spaniel who came into my life—thank you for forcing me to go on walks to observe the precious land of the elementals as I enter this most fascinating and exciting time of my life.

A special thanks again to Pamela for being ever at my side urging me forward with this project and helping me with the important initial editing and suggestions and prodding along the way. To Patricia Spadaro, who edited and helped shape the final versions of this book, allowing my voice to be heard and my words read. Thank you, Patricia.

Finally, I want to extend my gratitude to Hospice of Arizona. It was through you that I was able to pierce the veil and get a glimpse of the other side. To hospice workers everywhere— your work is inspiring not only for the client and their families, but also for those directly or indirectly connected to you.

CHAPTER ONE

A Perfect Stranger

"I hear you talk to angels."

Mary Lynne had found her way into my store, Angel Wings, during an art festival on the avenue one fall day. She was looking for an answer to a question she had wondered about for a very long time.

"A woman outside told me you could help me," she said, meeting my gaze with her deep blue eyes.

I waited and she began her story. She confided that when she was just a little girl, around the time her father had committed suicide, she began to see an angel in her bedroom. "The first time I saw the angel, I was five years old," Mary Lynne said with certainty in her voice. "It didn't hover, though I could hear wings flapping, and it didn't stand at the foot of my bed. The angel stayed just above my bedroom door. I know it was an angel—I just would like to know what kind of angel it was," she said, raising her eyebrows.

I knew right away that it was an angel of protection. "You

were in the angel's charge," I told her. "The angel was working hand in hand with your guardian angels, but this one had a specific job in your life at the time." She listened intently.

"This angel was there to soothe your aching heart, to mend the broken spirit of a frightened little who girl who had no one to turn to, no one to hold her or rock her," I continued. Mary Lynne nodded and then stared down at the floor.

"The angel of protection helped you feel safe in your room, away from the madness of the rest of the house—all the hollering, shouting, and threats of violence that were going on when you were a little girl. The angel helped you sleep on those scary, scary nights."

Tears welled up in her eyes, and she quickly wiped them away. "It was awful," she admitted, "all those fights. I always thought the angel's purpose was to protect me. I still hear the flutter of wings once in a while. I guess it's just a reminder that the angel's still with me." Mary Lynne slipped out of the store and into the crowd and I never saw her again.

Sometimes the visitors who stop and talk to me come for answers, but most of the time they just want to share. Somehow, they sense that I will listen, and listen without judgment.

Darby, for instance, a tall, gangly woman, walked right over to the counter where I was working and sat on the stool opposite me. I call this our spiritual bar stool. It's where so many customers sit and share their angel stories with me. She started making small talk, probing to see how serious I was about angels. After introducing herself to me, she removed her white-framed sunglasses and readjusted her sun visor atop her head. Then she got to the real reason she was perched across from me.

"Listen, I've got three granddaughters living in Bali, and

they all believe they have a guardian angel."

"Yes?" I said, knowing Darby had more to say on the subject.

"Well, what's peculiar about the whole thing is that my daughter and her husband have no belief system. Don't you find that a bit odd?"

"Not really," I replied, "since children just came from the spiritual world, what we often call heaven, and some of them still remember what it's like."

"Well, these girls talk to their guardian angels all the time, and their parents are livid! In fact, I just recently visited them and the three-year-old told me about her angel."

"And?" I asked.

"She told me that she had a guardian angel and pointed to the corner of the ceiling in her bedroom. Then she whispered to me, 'That's where my angel watches me at night time, Gramma.' "

With an inquisitive snarl on her face, Darby looked directly into my eyes and asked, "Now, how could they possibly know all of that stuff, never having heard about angels, let alone guardian angels, and without their parents ever talking about them and without these children ever setting foot in a church?"

Not waiting for a reply, Darby jumped off the stool, picked up her sunglasses, adjusted her sun visor and was gone as quickly as she had come in.

It happens like this all the time. People sit on that stool and look up into my eyes, hoping at last to unburden themselves of secret encounters they have kept inside for so long. "Well, you're a stranger, so I can tell you what happened," they say. They're afraid to tell a friend or relative for fear of being ostracized, so for weeks, months or even years and decades, they have remained silent.

But somehow, they know that here they are safe. They tell me of their near-death experiences and of seeing future events beforehand in their dreams. They tell me about seeing angels place their hands on the heads of their sick and broken loved ones as they pray in hospital rooms. They tell me of being in serious car accidents and having angels carry them miles away from the terrible wreckage, unscathed.

The people who come to Angel Wings sense that they can trust me. They know that although I'm a perfect stranger to them, I'm no stranger to the encounters or the crossroads that brought them here. You see, they're not the only ones who have encountered angels or seen coming events in their dreams. I have too. And if it can happen to me, it can happen to anyone, because I'm a very unlikely candidate, about as unlikely as they come. I was just a married guy with children who loved his season hockey tickets, climbed telephone poles for a living, came home from work, had an adult beverage and worked in the yard or on crossword puzzles.

We all have certain moments in our lives, knocks on our door, that are meant to wake us up, and the angels are involved in these awakenings much more than we realize. For me, it was a series of knocks. Not all of them were pretty, but all of them, I'm sure, were orchestrated by angels. They always had my best interests at heart, even when I thought that couldn't possibly be the case. I've come to learn that the angels can be trusted, because angels never lie.

The first knock began with a huge disappointment that still hurts when I think about it. My oldest son was graduating from an all-boys high school, similar to a college preparatory high school, called a Catholic minor seminary for religious reasons. The boys resided there throughout the week and went home on most weekends. Initially, many of the teachers were priests, but due to dwindling numbers of priests, lay teachers taught some classes.

My son's class turned out to be the last graduating class from the seminary because the newly installed bishop closed down the high school and it has never been reopened. Why? That's the million-dollar question that has not been answered in all the years since and perhaps never will be. Then again, it was a religious school, and religious institutions don't need to answer to anyone.

Those of us who were closest to the school, the dedicated parents, realized that the new bishop was going to bring down the hammer. We could feel it and smell it; we just didn't know when it would happen. Then, just three weeks before the end of the school year, the bishop announced to the news media—before telling anyone associated with the school, including the students themselves—that the school would be closed. The news came a bit late in the game for teachers and other employees to find new jobs since the next school year would start in less than three months.

The good man never could come up with a good reason for closing the seminary or for closing it when he did. Usually these kinds of closings occurred because of financial issues or declining enrollment, but in this case the seminary was financially self-sufficient with a growing enrollment. Pressed on the matter by concerned parents, the bishop reluctantly hired the firm of Meitler Consultants, Inc., of Milwaukee to evaluate the future use of the seminary building and grounds. The firm's report suggested leaving the seminary alone since enrollment was growing and it was self-sufficient, saying that the grounds could be updated for several other uses as well,[*] but the bishop shut down the school anyway.

Coming from a strongly religious family is one thing, but to see religion up close, warts, abuse and all, and working like a bottom-line corporation, brought many questions, rumors and too few answers. My son and the rest of the school's last graduating class all wanted either the rector (dean) or their principal to hand out the diplomas as they crossed the stage and made their final exit. Like all the other puzzling moves that preceded it, the bishop went against the wishes of the class and decided that he, and he alone, would hand out the diplomas to the graduating seniors. The majority of them, my son included, did not shake his hand.

The bishop felt offended, so offended that he was said to have remarked to the 122 priests in the diocese that these young men were not the kind of students the church needed. Most priests who were connected with the seminary disagreed with what he said. Privately, they sided with the students and parents, but officially they were loyal to the bishop. The other priests remained silent on the subject for fear of being reprimanded or asked to resign. The rector confided in me that he feared he would have to leave the priesthood if he disagreed with the bishop.

Some who were close to the seminary, including the rector, were privy to a letter the bishop wrote to priests in the diocese saying that the graduating class of 1995 was an embarrassment, not only to the diocese, but to the entire Catholic Church. During a mass the bishop celebrated at the seminary chapel, he

* See *They Were Children, Then* by Marge J. Brantmeyer.

even compared the situation to a family squabble, saying that from a spat will come a little unrest and possibly a divorce or two.

Maybe it does sound like a family squabble now, but the bishop's words hit me like a ton of bricks. I was devastated. I felt unjustly criticized and betrayed. My wife and I had raised the first of our three children to be an embarrassment to one third of the world? How did we do that? I thought we had spent eighteen years teaching my son how to be a good and decent human being. After all, he was chosen as the school valedictorian. He never missed a day of school from nursery school through high school, all of it spent in parochial schools. None of those students deserved such treatment from authority, especially religious authority.

For me, this event sparked a steady stream of questions, questions not just about the faith I had grown up in, but questions about life—questions I hadn't dared entertain before. I decided to take a time out from religion to contemplate the situation. After much thought and a few trips to the library to dig into the history of the religion I had been baptized into, examining the abuses of the recent past as well as long-ago sins spanning the better part of sixteen hundred years, I came to a conclusion. Rather than divorce myself from the church (actually it felt as if it had divorced itself from me), I simply resigned from formal religion. It wasn't an easy choice to break from my family's religion, but for me, there was no recourse.

Although it was years before I could forgive the bishop and the silent priests for what they had done, I have to thank them for bringing me closer than I could ever have imagined to God and the angels. Without that challenge, I may never have experienced the angels' intervention in my life or helped others to feel their presence. I may never have pierced the veil and seen into that realm some call heaven. Without that ugly situation, I may never have had the opportunity to help people learn about their loved ones who have passed over or been able to experience the presence of Mother Mary or Archangel Michael.

Since that time, so many have told me of their own encounters with angels, Spirit, Mother Mary, Archangel Michael, fairies and other phenomenon. Their stories are unfolded in these pages along with mine. In a way, they are my heroes for finally revealing the stories they held near and dear but had never been able to tell a living soul before. They are my heroes for confirming over and over again that there is indeed something bigger than us—that angels reside here too, standing next to us, guiding us every day.

Note: In my story and the stories I recount throughout the book, some of the names as well as minor details, such as names of cities or states, have been changed to protect the privacy of those who have been kind enough to share their stories of angelic and spiritual encounters.

Angels to the Rescue

"I have to tell you what happened to me thirty-five years ago," said Amanda, a petite woman who stood all of five feet tall and had dark brown hair and olive skin. "I left my house near the edge of town around 7 p.m. and drove to this little church eight miles out in the country. I was driving an older sports car at the time that did not have seat belts. After the church activities ended, I placed my purse, the dish pans and empty cookie sheet that I had brought to the event on the passenger seat. I got in the car and noticed how fresh the air smelled, so I decided to put the top down. I remember it being 9:45 p.m. as I headed down that old, winding back road on my way home.

"As I rounded a sharp turn on a dark stretch of the road, a deer suddenly jumped out and onto the road right in front of me. I swerved to miss it and the car went out of control, rolling over and over and over."

The next thing Amanda remembered was dreaming of being carried by an angel, who gently set her down five miles away from the accident next to an unlit building at a corner of an intersection where there was a pay phone. That's exactly where she found herself. In her hands, she was holding her purse with everything in it, the keys to the car, the pans and the cookie sheet.

"Now, how could I have possibly gotten out of that accident without a scratch and be five miles away at a pay phone with my purse, car keys and pans in my hands without an intervention from my angels?" she asked.

The next day, she returned to the site of the accident with friends, the sheriff and the tow truck driver to see her wrecked sports car. No one among them could figure out how she could have walked away from such a crash. Amanda knew. "As I stood there looking at what was left of the sports car," she told me, "a loving feeling washed over me, and from that moment on I have felt the 'ever presence' of angels. I have even named my daughter Angel."

I asked her, as I do with all those who share their accounts with me, if she would mind if I wrote down her story so I could share it with others. "Not at all," she said. "In fact, I want you to tell all of your customers and everyone you meet of the 'ever presence' of angels."

CHAPTER TWO

Crossroads

I returned from work to my home in south central Wisconsin one day to find a message on my answering machine. A representative of a telephone company in the southwest wanted to talk to me. More than four and a half years earlier, in sunny, warm downtown Phoenix, the same company had interviewed me. Now they were offering me a job in Mesa, Arizona. Having lived in Wisconsin for over forty years and having worked outside every day, freezing my tush off, the warmth of Arizona sounded appealing.

I knew it wouldn't be an easy move. Pamela liked her job and had a strong network of friends, both of which were hard to let go. Our daughter, Alicia, still had a year and a half of high school left. Our youngest, Curtis, had three years left at the same school, had just made new friends and felt settled in there. Brad, our oldest, was finishing his first year at a college just outside Chicago and wasn't too keen on the idea of us leaving him behind.

After several family discussions weighing the pros and cons, the move was on. We pulled up stakes and moved to the Valley of the Sun, leaving the frozen tundra and the snowblower behind.

Being from the upper Midwest, we were bound and determined to have certain things once we arrived in the desert of Arizona. Either we were highly motivated or just damned stubborn. We felt we had to have a house in a location that would benefit all of us in our own special way. Alicia wanted a house near a park that had a volleyball court. Curtis wanted to be near a basketball court and baseball diamonds. Pamela wanted a home with a spa and without levels or steps. I wanted to be near water and baseball fields and I wanted to have a swimming pool, desert landscaping and no yard to maintain. I was very tired of mowing grass.

Ask and ye shall receive. We found a place in the East Valley that would accommodate everyone's needs. It was the perfect setting. Perhaps the most perfect thing about the house was that our new street was named Crossroads Drive. At the time, we didn't realize that we had arrived at such a profound crossroads. We had no idea that our lives were about to change in a dramatic way. I didn't foresee the chains that would be removed, the cords that would be cut, freeing me from people, places, situations and old ideas and ideals. Standing at the corner of Crossroads Drive, I had not a clue of the life-altering events that were about to occur.

During the summer of '97 as I was driving along the highway that connects Phoenix and other cities in the southeastern part of the valley, I noticed a billboard with the most beautiful image of an angel I had ever seen. Her shimmering honey-blond hair was long and flowing. Her robes and her profile, all in a milky color, emanated grace, dignity and love. The sheer beauty of this angel caught me off guard. There was something about that billboard that moved me. It talked to me. As I glanced up at the angel, I wondered what it meant.

Two days later on the same stretch of road, I looked up at the billboard again, but this time I noticed the words *The Messengers*. The billboard was advertising a book about angels. It seemed to be a perfect birthday gift for Pamela, who had been reading a lot of stories lately. We hadn't been in the valley long enough to get to know others, so we both had plenty of time now for pleasure reading.

Pamela was reading three books at a time, and I bought her the angel book with anticipation. A week or two later, she was still reading all her other books. I was getting irritated and wished she would get on with *The Messengers* and put down those damned John Grisham books and the Stephen King novel (of course, I wouldn't damn Stephen King—I wouldn't want a hex put on me). After all, I had given *The Messengers* to her as a birthday present. All the wishing and hoping got me nowhere. Pam was going to read the other books first and there was no getting around it. So I started reading *The Messengers* one night and couldn't put it down. By the next night, I had finished it. That was record time for me.

Before *The Messengers,* I had only read three books about the "other side." In the mid-1970s, I read the groundbreaking book *Life after Life* by Raymond Moody. Then in 1992, I stumbled upon *Embraced by the Light* by Betty Eadie. During the upheaval at my son's school in 1995, I found myself reading Dannion

Brinkley's *Saved by the Light.* The books by Betty Eadie and Dannion Brinkley introduced pathways to a better way of life via near-death experiences and led people in the direction of a peaceful reuniting with God and Spirit. Pam read them too. They mildly intrigued me and gave me a feeling of wanting more. There weren't many books available back then on the subject of the afterlife and near-death experiences. My eyes were opened, however briefly, but my religious beliefs at the time successfully kept me in sleep mode.

That was all about to change. Soon I would fully allow myself to awaken to the reality of Spirit, angels and direct contact with them. I wondered, as I watched my growing interest in these subjects, if the old Buddhist saying could be true: When the student is ready, the teacher will appear. I think so, I told myself. I *am* ready. The sparks within my soul are ready for a gust of wind, a breath of life to turn them into a raging fire of learning. God, I am ready for you, for your word, for your angels. Lord, I am ready for the truth.

The story in *The Messengers* of Nick Bunick's involvement with the angels took me by surprise. Nick was not particularly devout in any religion, yet the angels intervened in his life. I had only heard of very religious people having visions or being in the presence of Jesus or the Virgin Mary, people like nuns, monks and Oral Roberts. And then I remembered those three books I had read about near-death experiences.

Finally, buoyed by my enthusiasm, Pam also read *The Messengers.* A month later we were at Changing Hands, a bookstore in Tempe, where Nick was doing a book signing. As he was signing Pamela's book, he turned to me and, in his soft voice, said, "I feel your energy."

Energy! How the hell do you feel energy? Little did I know at the time that the angel book and Nick's story would take me to places I had never been to, much less thought about. I would be meeting interesting souls, new age authors, lecturers and those who are known throughout the world for their gifts of insight and enlightened teachings.

Once I started reading about angels, I thirsted for more. The more curious I became, the more books I read. I had lots of questions. Are angels really with us all the time? Do they intervene in our lives? Can they come to anyone, even those who don't go to church every Sunday? Is there a hell? Can we have a conversation with God without formal prayer? Does God answer our questions? How? Asking these questions was like opening the door and inviting the angels to come closer—and that's exactly what they did.

Fairies, Flowers and Angels

Nora and her family live in the western part of Kentucky in a house tucked back in the woods on the outskirts of a midsized town. One beautiful January day while she was visiting with relatives, she came into Angel Wings and told me about her daughter's encounters with angels. The day after six-year-old Ashley's open-heart surgery, Nora was at Ashley's bedside, holding her hand as the little girl woke briefly and spoke.

"Mommy, there are six angels around me. Just before the surgery, one of them leaned down and whispered in my ear, '*You will be fine. Not to worry, little one.*'" With that, Ashley fell back to sleep on her hospital bed.

Two days later, as Nora opened the door to her daughter's hospital room, Ashley summoned her mother to her bedside. Ashley asked her to get closer so she could speak softly to her.

"Mommy," she said in a voice that was both questioning and matter of fact, "will you be honest with me?" Tears began to well up in Nora's eyes, not knowing what to expect.

"There really isn't an Easter bunny or a Santa Claus, is there?" her daughter asked quietly. "They aren't real, are they?"

When Nora asked why she was thinking about that, Ashley shared more of what she learned while in a sleep state during the surgery. She said that she had asked the angels who came to her during her operation if they were like Santa Claus or the Easter bunny. The angels replied that Santa Claus and the Easter bunny did not really exist but were folklore, intended to be part of the world of a child's imagination. But, they said, angels and fairies are the real thing.

Since that operation three years ago, the angels have never left Ashley. She tells her mom that she has six angels with her every day. Not only does she see angels, but she also sees fairies and other spirits too. Ashley says that once in a while, when the fairies are nearby, she can even smell the scent of shrubs and trees or the scent of flowers, sometimes bouquets of flowers.

After Nora finished sharing her story, she left the store with a serene smile, and I had one too. God bless, you, Ashley, for giving us a glimpse into the invisible beauty that is all around us and for affirming the existence of angels and fairies.

CHAPTER THREE

The Voice of an Angel

Pamela's father, Marlyn (Marlie) Gallagher, was scheduled to have a procedure to unclog the carotid arteries in his neck. The first operation went so smoothly that a few weeks later he decided, and his doctor agreed, to move ahead as soon as possible with the next part of the procedure. Part two didn't go so well.

Shortly after the operation, while in recovery, Marlie suffered a stroke. He was paralyzed from the neck down and couldn't speak. Pamela packed a suitcase and flew back to Wisconsin to be with her dad and the rest of her family. As she was leaving, she reminded me of a meeting I was supposed to attend the next morning. "Be sure to set your alarm so you can leave earlier than usual so you won't be late," she warned.

With Pamela back in Wisconsin, I had to fend for myself. The microwave oven and I came face-to-face for a few brief seconds. "Naw, I'll use the grill," I said, talking to myself. After feasting on a good old Sheboygan bratwurst and an iced tea, I took a swim in the backyard pool. Later that evening, I worked on a crossword puzzle, then turned out the light and tuned out the world.

As I lay asleep early the following morning, I suddenly heard someone call out my name.

"Gerald!"

I shot straight up, my eyes the size of grapefruits. It was the same voice my wife uses when she wants to get my attention. She says my name in a deeper tone and in that stern yet amusing way: "*Ger-rauld."* At the same time the voice and the name boomed inside my head, I was also hearing it outside my head— far above and to the right side of the bed to be exact.

Where, why and how did this voice appear? I looked around into the darkness all around me and then lay back down, pulling the covers up around my neck. I lay still but my eyes were darting everywhere—up, down, right, left. Everything looked normal. Glancing over to the alarm clock, I realized that I hadn't set it to wake up early for that meeting and it was time for me to get up and get going. But that voice! Where had it come from?

Still dazed, I climbed out of bed and stood at the place where I thought the voice had come from. I estimated that it had come from about a foot above my head and I'm six feet tall. Then suddenly it hit me like a ton of bricks. *It was the voice of an angel disguised in Pamela's voice or at least using her modulation. That dude had to be a big, tall angel.*

I stumbled off to the shower to get ready for the day, looking over my shoulder and shaking my head. All the way to the meeting I couldn't get that voice out of my head and I couldn't wait to tell Pam about it. Later that day after work, I called Pam to see how things were going in Wisconsin and to tell her about the wild angel encounter that morning.

"I heard a voice really early this morning," I told her. "I know this sounds funny, but I think it was your angel,"

"You know, it's funny," she said, "because I was sitting next to Dad and thinking about you and wondering if you had set the alarm or even remembered that you had a meeting to get to. Over and over in my mind, I was thinking about you just sleeping away and not getting up and I asked my angels to make sure you got up."

I listened with focused attention and then chimed in. "Then it *was* your angel that came to me this morning on your behalf!"

I felt Pamela reach out to me through the phone and squeeze my hand in nervous excitement.

"What did he say?"

"What you would have said if you were here and caught me sleeping through the alarm," I said nonchalantly and with a sheepish grin. "*Gerald* is what he said, and he spoke it like you would—*Ger-rauld.*"

She chuckled with her youthful playfulness and love. "I have very lovely angels that know my husband all too well."

"I guess! And extra large ones too," I shot back. "This guy had to have been about seven feet tall, because when I got out of bed and stood where I heard the voice coming from, it was a good foot above me!"

More chuckles erupted from Pam.

"See, I told you I was worried that you'd forget the alarm."

I felt my lips begin to purse. "Yes, dear."

I'd been reading about people who had had interactions with angels, but hearing that voice was my first affirmation that contact with the Spirit world and angels was possible—and that it was possible for me. Did I ask for proof? No. At least I didn't think I had. But I'll never forget it.

That playful display of spiritual contact was just the beginning. Every time I experience another one of those powerful encounters, I wonder: Was it me who made contact with these spiritual beings or they with me?

The next affirmation the angels sent me—"the correction," as I call it—came just a few days later. I was hanging family portraits on a wall in the living room. The top photo was a family portrait of my father and his three brothers with their parents. My ego, my lower self, was really fighting for position within me that day and it was winning. I looked at my grandparents and mentally started giving them hell. I didn't like the way they raised their kids. There were problems in that family, severe depression and alcoholism, just to name two. I blamed my dad's parents.

I continued hanging pictures, mentally laying it on both of them, when a big picture directly below their picture flew off the wall. I was wearing sandals and the corner of the frame landed right on the big toe of my left foot. Now I really had something to yell about. I swore, hobbled around and bled all over the place. The picture frame had cut through to the bone. I should have had stitches, but I was too embarrassed to tell anyone how it happened.

I found out something about the Spirit world that afternoon. Those who are on the other side don't get angry; they are beyond simple human emotions. But they do help illuminate truth in whatever way they can. Someone was correcting me and showing me the poor angle of my perspective. After the initial shock, I yelled at full volume, "Stay awake, Jerry!" The angelic forces in my life were calling me to do just that—wake up. I knew this was a wake-up call from God. I was beginning not only to listen, but also to hear within the inner chambers of my soul, within that special place deep inside and not far from the heart.

Those two events occurring so closely together helped me realize that Spirit is not to be taken lightly. We can deny the existence of Spirit all we want, but Spirit will not deny us. Spirit is as real as you and me, and there is no dividing line between it and us. We are all connected, and we have all the clues we need to participate in this journey of discovery if only we will listen and follow them.

I was awakening, I was starting to follow the clues and I was beginning a new journey. And what a ride it has been—a rollercoaster ride through the sky with angels holding on to me, keeping me from one helluva plunge. My rollercoaster car was now sweeping me toward another twist and turn, one called hospice.

Grandpa's Wink

My father-in-law, Marlie Gallagher, suffered a stroke in the recovery room after surgery and died six weeks later. Our son, Brad, shared with us this experience he had with his grandfather just before his passing.

"Grandpa and I became close while I was living with him and Grandma during summers and school vacations. He taught me how to hunt and fish and he would share war stories and accounts of hunting and fishing trips. He would also talk about Steel Forms, the construction company he started almost fifty years ago. He was involved with Steel Forms up until the day he had his stroke. I worked on an outside crew that summer that took the forms off the newly poured cement.

"Because of how active Grandpa had been, it was hard to see him in a hospital bed with all the tubes and hoses in him and to see him partially paralyzed. It hurt to see him that way, and you could feel and almost taste his pain and frustration.

"One summer night while he was sick, I had a dream. I dreamt that I was in the living room, kneeling next to Grandpa, who was sitting in his favorite La-Z-Boy. He wasn't lying back but was sitting upright, with both hands on the armrests. He was dressed in his usual attire, khaki slacks and a button-down shirt. He was clean-shaven and had his hair nicely combed back, as if he had just gotten out of the shower and was ready to meet the world. He had a pleasant look on his face and there was a glow about him. He seemed very content and didn't say a word.

"While I was kneeling beside him, he raised his left hand and started moving his fingers around and rolling his wrist a little. He had been paralyzed for over a month, so I looked at him in amazement and said, 'Grandpa, you can move your hand!' He looked at me with a grin and gave me his patented wink from his left eye. It was his way of saying everything was all right.

"I had gotten that same wink a couple of days before his stroke. After dropping off some supplies, he had started down the road in his blue Dodge and I waved at him. He smiled and gave me the same wink I saw in my dream.

"In the dream, after he winked at me, I heard the phone ring and I woke up. My first thought was that it was raining and my boss was calling to tell me not to come to work. Then I heard Grandma on the phone saying things like, "Oh, my God, really? I wasn't expecting this. Oh, God." So I knew something was wrong. I went out to see what happened, and after Grandma hung up the phone, she told me Grandpa had died.

"I didn't think of my dream until the next day. And for some reason, I've never cried when I've remembered it. Maybe it was because in the dream Grandpa had smiled and winked, telling me everything was all right. At least, I like to think so."

We buried Pamela's dad on August 2, 1997, on her sister's fortieth birthday. Her sister was having a difficult time with his death and prayed for a sign that he was okay and was with her. The day after the funeral, Pamela's sister, her husband and their three children went to a family camp in northern Wisconsin, as they had done for a number of years. That evening, as part of the program for the children, a man talked about birds of prey and showed them one special bird, a falcon, whose name was Marlie. Pamela's sister couldn't believe her ears and she giggled to herself. Then she strode right up to the man and asked for the name of the falcon again. Yes, it was Marlie. Her sister had received her sign.

Life has a way of communicating, sometimes secretly, sometimes obviously. If we pay attention, we will learn all that is necessary to continue along our respective paths toward enlightenment.

CHAPTER FOUR

Wanted: Good Home for Free Angel

I listened to my soul, followed my heart and took a plunge into the unknown. Most of my life, I had found myself volunteering for one thing or another. When I had just turned nineteen, I volunteered for the draft and spent two years in the army during the Vietnam era. Later, I coached youth sports and participated in Big Brother and Sister programs to help the needy. Now I was in Arizona working for the phone company with a schedule of irregular days and hours, making it difficult to volunteer for anything that required a specific time or day. I felt stuck.

Two years after we had settled into our new home, Pamela ordered an angel figurine through a popular catalogue we received semiannually through the mail. When the figurine arrived at our front door that summer, it didn't look anything like the one pictured in the catalogue. Pam wrote and asked if she could return it, expecting that she would either have to send it back or be stuck with it. The woman in charge of the customer service department wrote back that the company would indeed credit Pam's account, but instead of asking her to return the angel figurine, the woman told Pam to give it to a charity she felt would appreciate it.

I did a lot of driving as part of my work, so I volunteered to take the angel along with me. I thought that when I passed a place of interest, I would take the angel in to see if that might be her new home.

My first opportunity to find a good home for the angel was at a four-story office building in Mesa, where I had to do some work in one of the suites. The sign on the front of the building named all of its tenants. One stood out from the others—Hospice of the Valley. Hey, I thought, that's a possibility. I retrieved the angel from the front seat and headed toward the hospice suite.

I tapped on the door and walked in. Immediately to my right, I saw the front desk—a pet peeve of mine. Why is the front desk so often off to one side? You rarely walk right into a place and find yourself facing the front desk. Anyway, no one was there. I left, figuring this was not the angel's new home and that I would take her somewhere else. It didn't happen. That week nothing else stood out to me. No charity or helping-hand kind of place appeared on my route.

Midweek, at the end of my day, I found myself back at the building where the hospice office was located. I pulled into the parking lot and walked up a flight of stairs. The door was open this time and a young lady stood behind the front desk. She was bright, cheery and eager to take Pamela's angel. I asked if the angel could be put on a wall in a patient's room where she would be available to anyone. And so it was.

I couldn't get hospice out of my mind. With the radio on during the day, I would hear commercials inviting people to become a hospice volunteer. The same thing happened in the evening, but on television. Hospice ads were appearing everywhere. Whoever was really behind them, trying to reach me, was doing a good job. I picked up the phone, called three of the six different listings in the phone book for hospice programs and got the inevitable voice mail. A decorated old British general once said, "I don't hate anyone; I merely dislike them intensely." I dislike voice mail intensely. I put the phone down after the third voice mail and called it a day.

Only one of the programs ever returned my calls—Hospice of Arizona. I found out later that I wasn't the only one this had happened to. During a volunteer orientation session, the volunteer coordinator, Lisa, asked us why we had chosen Hospice of Arizona. Lisa sat at one end of two banquet tables placed lengthwise to accommodate our class of ten—nine women and one guy, me. I liked that. In answer to her question, we all spoke up at once and, almost to the very word, we all said, "You were the only one who returned my call." Every one of us had left messages with several hospice programs, including the one doing all of the advertising, but only Hospice of Arizona returned our call.

Could it have been coincidence? That would depend on your definition of that word. The dictionary describes *coincidence* as a sharing of the same place or time, happening at the same time or occupying the same position in space by chance. Judy Peters, who was the bereavement coordinator at Hospice of Arizona, has a much shorter and to-the-point definition. Judy is what I call an earth angel. The help she gives to patients in transition and their families is nothing short of angelic. According to Judy, coincidences are "small miracles that occur daily on an hourly basis."

One of the most intriguing aspects of the volunteer class was that I had a sense of "knowing" each of the other nine volunteers before meeting them. We all sensed some deep connection. For me, it was like a deja vu experience. I couldn't have known them in this lifetime, though, as we all came from some other part of the country before settling in the Southwest. Still, they felt like family.

Everyone at that orientation session became a certified hospice volunteer. We came from different backgrounds and different walks of life, from lawyers to teachers to retirees, yet we had at least one thing in common. All of us had lost a family member through diseases such as cancer, diabetes or Alzheimer's. I later realized that we had come together at that time in our lives through something more powerful than mere chance or coincidence. Maybe it was time for each of us to make a statement.

Part of the philosophy of hospice is to allow patients to be free from pain during the end of their lives, and we still felt the sting of having watched and tried to comfort our own loved ones who had died in pain because their doctors would only prescribe a controlled amount of medication. We felt that it simply didn't have to be that way and we wanted to help. It had seemed so unnecessary, so cruel. Our loved ones had been left to die alone in darkened rooms. Many times, they suffered weeks or months of agonizing pain before they crossed over. My own father was one of them.

My father, William Miles Van Slyke, and his three older

brothers before him all died of cancer, in pain and alone in a dark room at the end of an unlit hallway. My father was seventy-four years old.

My brother and I, along with our wives, had done all we could to help Dad in his transition and still he suffered for months in unrelenting agony. He was never able to find relief from the constant crawling slivers of mounting pain that did not remain slivers for long. The doctors could do no more for him than regulate the pain killer, morphine, that dripped from the IV bag into his veins.

The nursing home was forty-five miles away from where Pamela and I lived. She came home from her work and tended to our three small children and their needs while I drove almost every night after work to be with my dad. I stayed with him as long as I could, not knowing which night would be his last. On one particular Sunday, I was with him all day and late into the evening. He slept most of the time, but while he was awake he pressed the button for the morphine drip all he could. It still wasn't enough to stop the pain.

Late that April afternoon, as he was lying on his back and I was standing at the foot of his bed, he raised his head slightly. The light in the room, though dim, seemed too bright for him. He squinted and covered the brightness by putting his hand just above his brow, as if in a salute. His movement took me away from thoughts of my uncles and how they had died. His oldest brother, Ken, was the first to go, followed by the next oldest, Ralph. On the day of Ralph's burial, Lloyd died.

My dad began to tell me that he had just awakened from a dream where he was in a foot race with one of his nephews, who was suffering from heart disease. The winner got to die first. My father won the race. He grinned at the absurdity of it as he explained the dream to me. We had a chuckle at the idea of a foot race, though the levity of the moment was short-lived as he lay his head back down on the pillow and winced in pain.

My father did beat his nephew in that race toward death after all. He died in the early hours of the next day, after I was gone. When we saw him a few hours after his passing, he was clutching the cord for the morphine drip that tangled through the rumpled sheets and underneath his pain-racked body, still in a fetal position with his arms dangling over the bedrail. His hands had been searching for the morphine button, which he could not find and could not press, and he was tightly holding the cord. A nurse on duty said they had cleaned him up for us, as he had drowned in his own vomit in the end.

I stood at the foot of his bed, looking over his body, knowing that the poor guy could never get enough morphine to kill the pain. The nursing staff only gave the patients what each attending physician ordered, which was never enough. Tears streamed down my cheeks and dripped from my chin to the floor in a flood of emotions I couldn't stop. He was my father. The fact that his last moments were consumed by pain, confusion, doubt and disbelief rankled and disturbed me to the core.

Hospice was practiced in a few places at that time, but not in Wisconsin, where William had lived, fished, played baseball, worked, loved and died. If there had been a hospice program in the area, he would have been in it.

Hospice. One small word and one big, long definition. The word literally means to show kindness and generosity to strangers or to care for our fellow beings, offering them nourishment and refreshment. Hospice has a special way of caring for people with terminal illnesses as well as caring for their loved ones. It is a philosophy rather than a place. The focus is always on comfort, not the cure, emphasizing quality of life and not quantity. It does not subscribe to euthanasia. Death, like birth, is a natural process, and hospice helps patients make their transition free of pain and in their own time.

The main role of a volunteer is to be supportive and caring, allowing the primary caregiver to take a breather. So I became a switch-hitter. Friendly visits help ease the boredom, loneliness and social isolation patients can feel. I found comfort in the fact that my patients were always happy to see me, to see another face, hear another voice, opinion or story, or just be in the same room with another life force, a reminder of their own humanity. To clear their mind, heart and soul, the patients would share with me what they felt they could not tell their caregiver, many times intimate stories and secrets.

Hospice allowed me to make a difference. I experienced miracles through the years I worked with Hospice of Arizona, miracles that still have a profound impact on me today. I felt privileged to know these children of God in that most sacred time of transition from this life to the next. Often, emotion enveloped my soul, and my body was overwhelmed as I wept at the communion that took place, even if only for a moment.

Dad, your pain, although needless, has taught me well and brought me closer to the event of being human. I believe with my whole heart and soul that no one has to suffer before dying, regardless of any outmoded ideas of guilt, sin and pain that try to convince us otherwise. Thank you, Dad. I love you.

The Golden Angel

Irene walked into Angel Wings one day through the courtyard door. She was a big-boned gal in her early '70s. With her purse strap slung over her left shoulder, she clutched her purse like a football. Irene browsed through the store looking for that special gift for a dear friend of hers who was terminally ill with cancer. She found it in a little friendship angel figurine. As she stood at the counter, I could feel a certain tenseness in her and tried to set her at ease with conversation.

"Hi, nice lady," I said in a store clerk's voice. "I'm Jerry. Is there anything I can help you with today?"

"No, I just came in to purchase a friendship angel for my close friend, who is struggling with cancer." Irene straightened up and took a deep breath, then haltingly let it out. She did it again and this time her shoulders dropped as if she were letting go of a heavy load.

"You know, I'll tell you a little story," she said, hemming and hawing a little as her chest heaved. Then she shrugged her shoulders and added, "I'll tell you, but I've only told this to my husband, John. A few years ago, my mother passed away. My father had passed away years earlier and I was the only one left in our family. I had the only key to the house and went over every once in a while to do some cleaning and to take things to Goodwill.

"I'd been doing this for a couple of months and one time I noticed something that had not been there before. Sitting on top of my mom's dresser, as usual, was her jewelry box, but sitting on top of the box was a golden angel. My mom believed in angels, but I had never seen an angel in her house before. To this day, I don't know how it got there.

"I told that story to a neighbor, a dear friend of mine who is elderly and lives alone across the street from me, the friend with cancer. The strangest thing happened! After I told her the story of the golden angel appearing in my mom's room, she had a surprised look on her face. She reached into her coat pocket and pulled out a golden angel almost identical to the one I had found in my mother's house. 'I have one too,' she said. 'I recently found it in my pocket, and I don't know where it came from either!' "

CHAPTER FIVE

A Peek into Heaven

September in the Valley of the Sun is hot, 106 degrees in the shade. It had been well into the 100s since early May that year. I sat in my truck, parked underneath one of the few shade trees in Mesa, Arizona, gulping down ice water from my cooler and wiping sweat from my brow. Taking a well-deserved break, my mind wandered to my volunteer work.

The opportunity to instantaneously feel connected to other human beings as they were about to make their transition was awesome and rewarding. I thought about the three patients I had worked with in Arizona. The first had lung cancer. She kept a pack of her favorite cigarettes, Salems, by her bedside. The next one suffered from dementia along with lung cancer. He always wanted me to sneak him out of the hospital and get him a pack of cigarettes. The third patient suffered from heart failure and had the crazy idea that sharing his dreams with others would allow the devil to steal his soul. I had helped all three through their last days and wanted to help others. There was only one problem. Hospice hadn't called for months.

Already hot and bothered by five months of the desert heat, the steam was rising within as I wondered why I hadn't been assigned a new patient when so many people needed comfort. I thought about the fear people experience at the end, the vulnerability. Most of us had been taught all of our lives to fear God and feel the guilt of being born stained with sin, and we were reminded constantly of how hard it is to remove all sin from our souls to earn access to heaven. Thank you for that, O religious doctrine, as if we needed anything else to make us feel separate from one another or to cause fear to lay waste to hope.

Fortunately, God sleeps with one eye open. He understands our predicament—that our ego (lower self) has a tendency to create a dark side, away from our higher self, away from the light, from good, from God, and that this causes us to create our own ridiculous and unneeded problems.

I was still in the process of learning this, though. Inside, I heard myself talking through my anger and frustration, my voice raised and swearing a blue streak. The end of the one-sided conversation went something like "and as far as hospice is concerned, I *did* hospice, and I'm done waiting for them to call!" Before I could grab another drink of cold water, my cell phone rang.

"*Hello!*" I yelled into the phone.

"Jerry? This is Lisa, your hospice coordinator. How are you today?"

Without waiting for me to tell her how I really felt, she continued, "We have a new patient. At the meeting this morning, your name came up. Jerry, to be honest with you, we have called three other volunteers and they turned down this assignment."

"I'll do it," I heard myself say without hesitation. After all, I was on a rampage to help ease the emotional pain of others during their last days in this world.

"His name is Eddy and he just turned 31," Lisa said. Her voice seemed to be far off and yet direct. "Eddy has a very rare cancer. His stomach and much of his intestines have been removed and he has two bags that his new bride of six months is tending to every few hours."

I swallowed hard. "How long has Eddy been sick?"

"His illness was discovered three months ago and he has already lost over 160 pounds. His wife, Angela, has to wear a mask when changing out the tubes and emptying the bags." I immediately knew that it was time for me to contribute in any way possible.

"I'm your man, Lisa," I said. Still feeling a bit angry, I took over the conversation now, asking her to give me Eddy's phone number and send me the usual information packet. I hastily jotted down his number on the back of an envelope.

"Jerry, just remember that if you decide not to take this assignment, we would all understand," Lisa said. I stuffed the envelope into my sweat-soaked shirt pocket, drove back to the company's facilities and called it a day.

Later that evening, feeling rested and cool in the friendly confines of home, I took out the envelope with the name and phone number of my next hospice assignment and dialed the number. I spoke with Eddy's wife, Angela, and set a time to meet at their apartment in Phoenix the following Saturday morning at 10 a.m., the first Saturday I had had off in months. Angela handed the phone to Eddy and we spoke briefly. I don't remember much of the conversation except that he sounded pleasant and easy going. It was autumn in most of the rest of the country and we talked sports. He professed to being a die-hard Pittsburgh Steelers fan.

As I lay down on the cool sheets of the bed that evening, kissing Pamela goodnight and feeling thankful for the breeze of the ceiling fan, I told God how good it felt to be back working with a hospice patient. I apologized for my anger and inability to accept that I was working on God's time and not God on mine. I also asked God about the books on the afterlife that I read recently and if I should pursue more books on spirituality. I remember kissing Pamela one more time, on the back of her neck, and quickly falling into a deep slumber.

Sometime during the night, I was transported to a place I had never visited before and have never visited since. I found myself standing in front of a man who was instructing me. At first, I was watching the events as if I was outside of myself, viewing myself from behind. Then I was able to watch the events take place from any angle. At times, it felt as if I was in a Disney World theater watching the scenes on a big screen with surround sound. I was seeing everything from a 360-degree panoramic view. Where was I? A place called heaven.

My teacher's face was bright pink. His entire being glowed like a newborn babe wrapped in a white aura. He was on the tall side, maybe six foot two. I saw an outline of a goatee and noticed that he was balding. His hair was no longer than half an inch in length on the sides and had receded far back atop his crown. As I looked at him speaking, I realized that this being of love was on a higher plane than I and in another world. As we stood face-to-face, I saw myself in black and white, while his world was alive with brilliant colors, emanating an immense feeling of flowing, blissful peace and love.

Around the teacher, as far as my eyes could see, floated translucent beings of light, cherublike and smiling, that I interpreted to be angels. I could see through them. They had wings and were in flight, although their wings didn't move. Awestruck, I gazed around in wonderment. The grass was as green as the rain forests of Hawaii or maybe greener than any on earth. The grass spoke to me. As I became aware of the trees, their branches and their leaves, I could sense their energy. I heard and understood the intonations of all life.

The grass, trees, flowers, animals and even the molecules spoke to me and shared insights with me. My boundaries stretched, my ego dissolved and there was no duality, no separateness. I felt that I was a part of all things. Sometimes the communications came in word form and sometimes they came as a transparent bolt of energy that downloaded information into me from all that I was seeing and feeling.

Before I could actually form a question, it was answered. Instantaneously, my thoughts, including assumed facts, were either affirmed or corrected. For example, I wanted to know about the Bible and a question was forming in my mind as to its accuracy and intent. I received this answer:

Except in the minds of people, it does not matter. However, as an answer for you to share with others, the Bible is incomplete. There were more authors dedicated to writing in order to enlighten. Their intention was to write many books for the purpose of leading all the peoples of the world out of the darkness of unconsciousness and into the loving light of God. The writers also knew that their writings had to be protected and kept out of the hands of the pow-

erful and political peoples of that time and times to come or these works would either be rewritten for their personal interests and gains or be destroyed altogether. Many of the original writings were edited out of the book you call the Bible.

All the manuscripts were once intact. However, today many sit deteriorating in Rome. The so-called Dead Sea Scrolls as well as the writings called the Nag Hammadi Library were meant to be part of the Bible. The Bible, the Nag Hammadi texts and the Dead Sea Scrolls were all written by the same authors and were meant to be handed down to all generations to come. The writings on those scrolls have been in the hands of many scholars and have been translated and published. These translations are now available throughout our planet Earth and rest on the hearths of those with varying religious beliefs.

Yes, much of the Bible was rewritten at the directives of high officials of the time to serve the purposes of translators or because of misunderstanding between languages. Parts of what is recorded in the one version you are familiar with are intact. In spite of changes, it is safe to say that "there is some truth in all religions." Scholars who study the writings know what is truth and what has been altered. However, sometimes they let the dogmas they follow interfere with their findings.

My attention returned to my new surroundings as the heavens showcased themselves. The grass was saying to me: *With a greater love than you can know do I allow you to use me to hold your balance and stand your ground. I willingly allow you to walk upon me as the love of my angel stands behind me.* Then, as I gazed upon the beautiful green grass, I noticed that behind each blade stood a deeper and more intensely colored blade that was rounder and taller than the straight and narrow one in front of it. It became clear to me that each blade of grass had an angel of its own standing right behind it. The grass continued its communication: *Breathe in the oxygen that I offer up for you.* The grass I was not standing on gently swayed, the thinner blades moving melodically in unison with the deeper, rounder blades of grass behind them and emitting a deep sense of peaceful joy. Not just the grass, but everything around me swayed to and fro in unison.

Harmonics permeated all of this heavenly world, and there was music in everything and everywhere. Music could not only be heard but also be seen. I could choose to hear it, see it, feel it or use a combination of any or all of these senses to absorb it. It was that way with everything: words, sights, smells, thoughts and feelings of all manner and minutiae. All things were alive and they all had a higher frequency and vibrational quality or quotient attached to them—from rocks and flowers to trees, birds, animals, fish and oceanic life, air and people. I realized that not just the grass but all things had a bigger, brighter being of love right behind them. Everything was a loving, harmonic, peaceful existence, each with its own angel.

Colors were magnified tenfold. Even the various hues had music in them. Although the music surrounded everything and was everywhere, it wasn't in a way that I could describe precisely with words. Somehow, some way, words define, limit and cause boundaries to be built. What I experienced knows no separateness. It was unity, beauty, truth, all united in a feeling of peaceful, loving bliss. It was a quiet, serene blending of sight, sound and feeling within that beautiful, majestic place we call heaven.

At one point, my teacher spoke to me with a stern manner,

saying: *What I say is for you. Listen well. God is all. God is one. God is, was and will forever be a universal Love. There is only one God, who is not held to any religion and who is ever expanding and in everyone's thoughts, words and actions. God, like silence, cannot be divided. God lives within each spirit, each soul, and is everywhere at all times. The truest of the true master teachers cleared their hearts of all negativity and ego-based thought before they saw the light, before they saw the good, before they saw God.*

I listened to his words, but they were difficult to comprehend because I could not give him my undivided attention. I could not keep from taking in all there was to see. I did my best to focus on my teacher, but so much learning was happening. I was gathering knowledge from everywhere—from my teacher's words and actions, from the surrounding environment and from places the naked eye could not see within this ethereal world.

The knowledge that entered my body was vibrating through me. It came from the past, the present and the future—all in the now. Down through the layers of my skin, through my organs, I was being bombarded and penetrated by units of information at an infinite speed. My body made a sizzling noise as it absorbed the bytes of data traveling into and throughout my cells. Some of the data that went into the cells was information as to the cell's makeup, how life is formed and how to keep it alive.

As the knowledge entered my being and passed through me, I felt exquisite bliss. While my teacher spoke, I could also see the information he was conveying in 3-D in what seemed like fragments of a movie. I was learning that when we pass on from our life on earth and transition to this place, we receive a 360-degree panoramic life review. I was allowed to watch in 3-D some of

these life reviews. When I viewed these snippets, I
feel simple gestures of kindness that those in the li
conveyed toward others in their lives. I could als
and suffering that they placed on others with their unkind
thoughts, words and actions.

I learned that those who were inflicting pain on others were
also suffering and in pain themselves. The interesting thing
about their pain and suffering was that it was self-inflicted. They
had become angry because they saw in others what they had
chosen not be, or they saw in others a part of themselves that
they were unhappy with, something they had yet to resolve.
The anger wasn't about what someone else had done but was
caused by something within the observer himself.

If you prefer to call the life review "judgment day," so be it.
There is more to it, though. We get to see and feel the good, the
love and the kindness we have passed on to others as those people felt it, and we get to feel the rippling effect of our actions as
those people went on to influence their friends and loved ones.
During our life review, we also see and feel the anger, hate and
all the negative emotions we placed on others, and, again, we get
to experience it exactly as those individuals did at the time it
happened. Trust me, it's not pleasant. After my teacher showed
me this lesson in general terms, by seeing examples of the life
review, it was my turn. He gave me a small taste of my own life
review to ponder and swallow.

My teacher showed me instances in my everyday life where
I had erred and where I had made better choices. For example,
I saw myself as a teenager near a city bus stop in Kenosha,
Wisconsin, where I had lived, waiting to get on a bus as people
were getting off. A woman in her thirties was stepping down

from the bus and we made eye contact. Feeling insecure, as teens often do, I looked away. I was shown that if I had smiled or nodded, or both, it would have made her day a pleasant one. Instead, the poor woman was fighting depression and my looking away made her feel unwanted and unloved. Now I had to feel the impact of my reaction, as if I was she, and it didn't feel very good.

I was also shown the consequences of my loving actions, such as an incident that happened on a cold Wisconsin winter day as I was walking home from elementary school with a classmate. I was nine at the time. Temperatures were below zero and my friend was shivering and wiping away tears from his eyes with his cold bare hands. It was not a time to be without a winter coat and gloves, yet he had neither. He came from a large family with little income, and his clothes, like many in those days, including mine, were hand-me-downs. As we approached my house, I took off my coat and gave it to him, saying, "You keep it. Tell your mom I don't need it anymore." With a startled look, his face turned beet red. His eyes teared as he stared at it. He quickly pulled on the coat, wiped his eyes and nose with the back of his hand and walked on to his house several blocks away. This experience felt good—a warm, loving, blissful, overwhelming good.

When the good things in my life were brought to me for review, I was in absolute bliss. So, too, were the surroundings, the fish, the other animals and the plant life—everything. We could all move and sway as one because we could all feel the same loving desire to move as one happy family, and so we did. It was as if there was a deeper connection and we were long-lost relatives just uniting for the first time in eons. All of us there could feel the soft yet powerful unconditional love in our midst. It was magnificently incredible, like God's love shining upon us.

What about religion? Even before the thought fully formed in my mind, I saw myself turn back to my teacher. He was giving me instructions yet his lips were not moving. He was transferring the information to me telepathically: *Exclusive religions are not the way God intends religion to be. God lives in all people and all things at all times, in our conscious and unconscious thoughts, individually and collectively. God is what we think before we think it. God is ever expanding, and God's thought as it is now will change and a broader picture of God will enwrap the worlds. God is everywhere and in everyone. God is I. All living entities participate in this creative dance called life.*

This confirmed what I had learned earlier in the dream, that the Bible was just one of several of God's teachings and was not the first. For instance, the Buddha lived about five hundred years before Jesus and his words were written down. The same is true of Krishna and other ascended masters. Without having to ask, all the questions I had about God and religion were answered. The light, God and good are all one and basically mean the same thing—love and honor. Before God, there was the word *good*, and it was God. God was in the light; therefore light is good, God is good. I understood that all are one.

I learned that Jesus walked the earth as a master, a teacher and a healer. The Essenes and others taught Jesus (Yeshua) throughout his life. They taught him about his place in the world, his mission, when he was a child. He visited many areas, where he learned teachings in tongues other than Hebrew. Who he really is is not limited to the Jesus of the Bible. His ego was not and is not so large as to say, "The only way to heaven is through me."

I learned that there are many masters and many guides. As a master in his own time, Jesus taught that all people are to be included in the world of higher living. He showed to all mankind the way to love, truth and harmony so that all God's children could live together peacefully—so that all people throughout the world could have the chance to know inner peace, inner strength and a love greater than previously known to mankind. By divorcing ourselves from our lower selves, the ego, we can more easily be in touch with our higher selves, our Mother-Father God that resides within.

I learned that there is no *place* called hell. Hell is a state of mind. It is how people live without love, without the light, without God. Hell is the acceptance of duality, of good and evil. One may ask, "If there is no hell, where does all the evil come from? People murdering innocent people is evil. Where does the ugliness come from?" Like the emotion called hatred, evil is a creation of the ego (lower self) of man. It comes from the ego and the minds of ungodly people who have been taught by self-professed teachers with an incomplete knowledge of God or perverted ideas of what God wants. God is love, that's all. Since God is love, there is nothing else but love in God. There is no duality and there is no anger, no hatred, no apathy. God is all-inclusive and is made of whole, complete, pure, sweet unconditional love.

I learned that our connection to the earth plane is profound. We are all connected with our surroundings. The trees, rocks, grass, air, plants and animals are all made of the same structure and their DNA is not so different. Their molecules and ours are not very different either.

On our journey to be one with God, some paths have more curves and turns than others. But our purpose here is simple: to love. To emit love, radiate kindness, embrace, enfold, extend love to ourselves, to the others we meet and to those we have not yet met. When we can make our path straight, we will be one with God. It is not likely to happen in one lifetime. Only a small handful of people have done that and they are called masters.

My teacher told me that I would forget much of the message I had received but that when I would hear or see the truth, I would know it as truth. He said I would also know what was not the truth and I would be able to differentiate between the two.

I feel the love from that dream as if it occurred last night. Yet it took me several years to write down all the details. Why? For one thing, I didn't have to. The dream was and still is etched deep down inside my soul. None of it has gone away.

Before this dream, I looked at everything more or less from one dimension—from the perspective of my thoughts and my thoughts alone. After this profound, life-changing experience, there was no going back. The old thought patterns had been erased. The dream removed all my questions about the hereafter, heaven, God and religion. It was filled with affirmations, with wonderment and awe, and with an understanding of the purpose of life. Yet this peek into heaven was but a tiny spark of insight for new beginnings. It let me know that I'd just begun my journey into higher consciousness. What I didn't know at the time was that this was the first of a series of three dreams that would bring important changes into my life—and that the work of the teacher was only beginning.

A Love That Will Never End

"Can you tell me if my grandmother is an angel?" asked the tall woman with a shock of long black hair. Kendra had popped into Angel Wings with just one goal in mind—to ask me that question. Then, speaking more softly, she added, "I'm quite sure she went to heaven, she was such a kind woman.'"

"Well, in my opinion," I said, "generally speaking, I think most grandmothers are angels in every respect."

"No, no, I know that. What I mean is that all my life I was taught that only Christians could go to heaven. The grandmother I'm talking about is my husband's mother's mother. I was raised Catholic, but she's of Arab descent and she was such a sweet and loving woman. She lived to a ripe old age before passing on last year. She meant so much to me. I loved her dearly ever since my husband introduced me to her while we were still dating. She took to me right from the start and she taught me a special kind of love and how to be accepting of everyone."

She paused, looked directly into my eyes and said, "Well, you're a stranger, so I can tell you what happened."

Kendra sat down on the stool across from the counter where I was working and began her story. "One night last month while I was sleeping, it was a Tuesday night, I opened my eyes and there she stood, right at the end of the bed. She had a bright glow about her and her skin was a radiant color. She was wearing beautifully flowing garments and looking very young.

"My grandmother just stood there looking at me with a peaceful smile as I lay in bed. I was stunned! Here's the thing, I know I was awake because I reached up and turned on the light. When I did that, my grandmother disappeared—or at least I couldn't see her. Then I turned off the light and she reappeared. So tell me, angel man, is my grandmother an angel?"

"If you believe she's an angel, then she is," I said. "She may not be a winged angel, but she is there with the angels in the Spirit world, a space we call heaven. And you know she came to you because of the love you two shared. Your love is so powerful that it continues on, even though you live in this world and she lives in the Spirit world. Your grandmother knows your heart and she knows your love. She loves your very soul so much that she came to visit you.

"For you, it was a reminder of many things and an affirmation that you were right all along—*all* people can go to heaven. Our religion doesn't matter to God. You have love in your heart and so did your grandmother. Love is what counts. If you have love, you have God—you are a winner. The vision you had was an affirmation that your love will never end, no matter where you are, no matter where she is."

CHAPTER SIX

The Teacher Appears

The following morning, Friday, I awoke to another average day of work. It would surprise me, though, if I had gotten anybody's phone to work that day. I was in a heavenly daze. The whole day, the dream from the night before played and replayed in my mind. I tried to make sense of it all but could not.

The memories of the messages I had received, imbedded within me, appeared before my mind's eye in waves. *God resides in the collective consciousness of all people. The good, God and light, mind, body and spirit are all connected, are all one.* My head was still spinning over that one. I remembered seeing little orbs of loving life energy looking over young parents on earth and choosing them to be their parents, an insight I really liked. *The key to life and maintaining life is within us. God is singular yet is in all things and in all people all the time.*

As I lay down on the cool sheets that night, my dream was still rolling through my head like waves rushing ashore at high tide. The world in my dream had all the appearances of looking and feeling more real than the life that surrounded me.

The next morning, as the sunlight made its way through the bedroom window, penetrating through my eyelids, I awoke gently. I stretched with a slight grin, realizing that it was Saturday and that I didn't have to go to work. Pamela was already out of bed and in the kitchen. I could smell the bacon frying in the pan. Rolling over on my right side away from the window, I suddenly remembered that today I would meet my new hospice client, Eddy Cooper. How bad could it be? A bag or two—big deal, nothing to sweat, I've seen worse.

I drove into Phoenix with the directions in one hand and the steering wheel in the other, found the apartment complex and parked my car in the parking lot. With the apartment number in my head and the hospice volunteer bag over one shoulder, I walked the narrow sidewalk through the complex, looking for Angela and Eddy's place. Even though it was unseasonably warm, all the doors were shut except one, the one I was looking for.

As I collected my thoughts, preparing for the usual introductions and initial greetings, an image of the teacher in my dream came to me in vivid color. I brushed it away. There was no time for that right now. Rapping on the screen door, I peered in and saw a woman in her mid-twenties, plump and blond, approach the door. She seemed helpful and sincere.

"Oh, hi. Come on in. I'm Angela," she said.

"Hi, Angela. I'm Jerry, the hospice volunteer—" Angela interrupted to explain that she was just changing IV bags for Eddy and motioned for me to come in.

I opened the screen door and stepped into the living room of the small two-bedroom apartment. On the left, I saw a brown couch, and at the far end of it, in a dull white bathrobe, sat my client. He watched as I entered.

"Hi. You must be Eddy," I said. "I'm Jerry from hospice."

"I know. Come in," he said, extending his right arm for a handshake. Eddy's hand was quite warm and, like the rest of his coloring, ashen. A tall, thin man, his skin sagged around his waistline, a hint that he had once weighed much more and had lost a good bit of his weight during this recent ordeal. His demeanor was pleasant, unobtrusive. His eyes smiled as he looked me over in an investigative way.

I noticed that Eddy's light brown hair was receding on top and he had only about a half an inch of hair growing on the sides of his head. Suddenly, my mind exploded with flashbacks from my dream. *That's him—my teacher! Eddy was the teacher in my dream,* I thought, my mind racing.

"Have a seat," he said graciously. As I did, I could feel my heart pounding a hundred miles an hour against my rib cage. My neck stiffened, my body began to sweat. At the same time, a voice in my head was telling me to remain calm. *Remain calm? How the hell do I do that after realizing this guy is the teacher from my dream?* Grasping at straws, I tried to understand, knowing all the time that Eddy must be a central figure in my life and that he had a message to convey if only I would listen. "Be still and take this all in," the voice in my head continued. "There is more for you to witness."

Uh-oh, I thought. The word *witness* was a little foreign to me. From what I knew, it was used mostly in a religious way and it made me uncomfortable. Just as I was hearing these messages, I remembered what my teacher had told me at the end of the dream—that I would not remember all that had been told to me, but that I would have a knowing of what was and was not true. From then on, I just sat back, soaked up the scene and waited patiently for any or all of the miracles to come. There were many.

Eddy and I made small talk. He had been born in Michigan, though he had lived most of his life in Florida before moving to the Phoenix area. He was thirty-one years old, had never been to the ocean, worked in landscaping and was a Pittsburgh Steelers fan. I asked him how he knew about hospice. Angela, who was in the kitchen washing the dishes, overheard and interjected, explaining that she worked long hours, could not always be with him and needed a break. Eddy said he just wanted some company. He then leaned toward me and said in a hushed voice so that Angela could not hear, "I like to talk sports once in a while, too."

His deceased mother's sister as well as his two brothers lived in Phoenix, but they had stopped coming by when Eddy got sick. Angela's mother lived two hours north of Toronto, Canada, and had never seen or met Eddy because she couldn't afford a plane ticket to Arizona.

A football game was on the television and the Steelers were playing. We watched the game. The Steelers won. It looked as if his favorite team was on a roll as his body was giving out. Eddy never told me what his connection was with the Steelers, why it meant anything to him whether they lost or won. But for four Sundays in a row, we watched the Steelers win their games and all the while Eddy seemed quite satisfied.

When I came for my visits, Angela, ever the dutiful one, would usually be tending to Eddy or be in another room doing the laundry, folding clothes or washing the dishes and extra sets of Eddy's tubes and bags. It seemed she always had something to do that kept her busy in the house. Whenever she had to don her surgical mask, open Eddy's robe and change out the tubes and bags, she did it without complaint. The odor was not pleasant, nor were the tasks of emptying, replacing, washing and cleaning the surgical openings within his deteriorating body. Angela was an earth angel living up to her name, performing her angelic works on her newlywed groom of six months without a hint of reservation or hesitation.

My first visits with Eddy went by with no real surprises until the weekend of the third week. The day began with Eddy, his young bride, Angela, and me—just the three of us. Today we were all in the living room, watching the football game together. The play had stopped and the announcers said they would be right back after a few messages. There was a pause of a few seconds before the commercials started, a rare few seconds of silence on the television.

Suddenly, the screen door opened and in walked Eddy's aunt. His two brothers were right behind her. Lots of hugs, tears and apologies followed in this poignant and touching reunion. Except for Angela's mother, what few relatives Eddy had were gathered together in the tiny living room hugging each other. Eddy forgave everyone, embraced them all, told them that he loved them and thanked them for coming.

As I watched the reunion unfold, Eddy's aunt pulled out a framed picture of his late mother and put it just under the television, as if placing it strategically so that his mother would be able to see her son as he gazed at her image. It was her high-school graduation picture and in it a brownish-golden colored aura encompassed her head. I had never seen an aura around someone in a graduation picture before and wondered how it got there. Curious, I asked Eddy's aunt if the aura around her was placed there as a special effect or if the picture had always been like that.

She told me that the original didn't look that way, but she had just gotten a copy of it made that morning and that is how it turned out. I reached into my volunteer bag and pulled out an autographed copy of Dr. Doreen Virtue's book *Chakra Clearing: Awakening Your Spiritual Power to Know and Heal*, which Doreen had given me at one of her Angel Therapy workshops in Phoenix. I scanned through it until I came to the section on auras and her interpretation of the colors and their meanings. It read: "*Dark brownish yellow or gold: A student, or one who is straining at studying; overly analytical to the point of feeling fatigued or stressed; trying to make up for 'lost time' by learning everything all at once.*"

By this time, Eddy's aunt was sitting in the chair next to me. I gave the book to her and said, "Read this, if you will, and tell me if it has a connection to your sister's picture."

She looked down at the book and back up to me. I could see in her eyes that she was puzzled. She pulled the book onto her lap, studied it carefully and then drew it closer to read. Her eyes drifted away from the pages to focus on the graduation picture. With measured words, she said, "Yes, she was very worried during the picture-taking because of her poor grades and a test that she had taken prior to the graduation ceremonies. She was under a lot of pressure, could not study at home the way she wanted to and was afraid of failing the test." Eddy's aunt sat with her left elbow on her knee, her hand covering her slightly opened mouth as she stared in awe at her sister's picture, trying to comprehend what she had just read. I placed the book back in my bag, looked up to the ceiling, took a deep breath and then exhaled slowly. *Thank you, God, for affirmations received,* I said silently to myself.

I got up, waved to Eddy, who was standing between his brothers, said that I would stop back in a few days and slipped out of the tiny apartment and the tearful event. As I stepped outside into the light, I raised my arms, stretched my fingers, tilted my head back and, with a little smile glazed upon my lips, uttered, "Thank you."

The following Sunday, Eddy and I were watching another football game. His Steelers were winning again. Then the screen door opened and, once again, in walked his aunt and two brothers. This time, they had their significant others with them. Angela and Eddy were thrilled. It was time for me to leave them alone, or so I thought, when we heard a light rap at the door. A nurse from Hospice of Arizona appeared in the doorway and simply said, "I have someone with me who would like to see her daughter and meet her new son-in-law."

You could have heard a pin drop. Everyone looked intently at the caseworker as their mouths dropped open in shocked surprise. I had goose bumps. Eddy, who was seated, looked up toward the door as a brown-haired, petite woman with an athletic build peered from behind the nurse. Walking directly to him, she gracefully and gently bent down, reaching through the tubes and monitors to give Eddy a hug as he greeted her with outstretched arms. It was a long and loving embrace. Once again, not a dry eye in the house. I looked at the nurse and she at me. We had done our job for the day and it was time for us to go.

"Amazing! Absolutely amazing!" I said as I got up to leave. Feeling blessed to be able to watch the unfolding of such beauty and grace, love and honor, I was absolutely beside myself, overwhelmed by the energy flowing around me. I shook my head and looked skyward, sensing a deep connection to the angels I couldn't see but knew were there.

"Another miracle, huh?" said the nurse as we walked out of the apartment.

"I guess," I muttered, still in a state of disbelief.

"Let me tell you the rest of the story," she added, "because what we saw was just the finale of a string of small miracles."

She went on to explain that hospice keeps a small amount of money for emergencies, such as helping families make connections and a hotel room for a night or two. "Right now, our funds could not support a roundtrip airline ticket from Toronto to Phoenix plus room and board. One of the women in our department has a friend who works for an airline, so she called her to see if the airline could help out with a lower airfare. They offered to reduce the fare, but the cost was still too high. The woman who worked for the airline said that if the prices dropped, she would tell her friend at hospice." There was another problem, the nurse told me. In order for Angela's mom to get to Toronto, she first had to catch another plane at a small airport located an hour from where she lived, an added cost that neither she nor hospice could afford.

The woman who worked for the airline happened to be picking up another friend of hers at a travel agency for lunch and she was telling the travel agent about Eddy's situation. A man at the counter overheard the conversation and asked if they could get the hospice coordinator on the phone.

"It took some doing," the nurse said, "but the women managed to get the man and the hospice worker connected. To make a long story short, the man offered to foot the bill. He said he would pay for all the transportation needs for Angela's mom, he would put her up in the closest hotel to Angela and Eddy and he would pay for the food—all under one condition. His name was never to be mentioned."

Eddy's cancer was spreading quickly and his organs were giving out. Just three weeks after I had met him, his condition worsened to the point that Angela could no longer keep up with his increasing needs and he was moved to a nursing home. The first weekend he was there, I paid him a visit. As I entered the doorway to his room, I saw all of his family gathered around him. Angela looked up and greeted me. "Thanks for coming by. We need a little break," she said. One by one, she and the others left the room. After the last person had gone, Eddy picked up the television remote. He clicked once and the Steelers were at it again.

Although he was extremely weak as he lay in bed, he still managed to extend his right hand for the customary handshake. Instead of taking his hand, I sat on the edge of the bed, leaned over and embraced him. His voice, once strong, had been reduced to a whisper, but he managed to tell me that Pittsburgh was winning again and asked me to stay and watch with him. I stayed as long as I could and when his family returned, I said, "Well, your family is here now, so I'd better be going, but I'll be back next Sunday for the game." Unusually silent, Eddy's eyes found mine and he said softly, "They have a bye next Sunday."

He was right. The Steelers did indeed have a bye. From the

first time we met, the Steelers had won every game we watched. On that next Sunday, the bye week, at age thirty-one, Eddy died. He passed on from this world, surrounded by his loving family, not exactly content with life but surely ready to meet it head on. He told me once that although he wasn't a religious person, he did believe in God and Jesus and he wasn't afraid to die. And, hell, if his Steelers could fight the good fight, so could he.

I stopped back at the nursing home a few days later to talk to those who had cared for him. The entire nursing staff told me that they had never had a patient who was so pleasant. In fact, *he* was the one doing the comforting. He never complained, always greeted the staff with a smile and kind words, and even asked if he could do anything for them. That was how he was. He took life as it came, graciously. A living saint, an angel, he provided the strength for those around him, even though he was the one who needed care and was seemingly dependent. Everyone on the nursing staff said he was the best patient they had ever had.

All I know is that Eddy came to me in a dream two days before I met him. Both in the dream and in real life, he was my teacher. Eddy was a teacher to everyone. He taught gratitude, humbleness, appreciation of the little things and unconditional love. He taught thankfulness, too, for whatever time he had remaining in this world.

Thank you, Eddy Cooper, for coming into my dreams, for kick-starting my spiritual life and for teaching me compassion, gratitude and unconditional love. Your energy lives on because of the way you touched those around you. You did it by simply being yourself, Eddy, no more, no less. By living well, you were able to die well and pass from this life unfettered. Thank you again for allowing me to be a part of your life. And by the way, though it didn't happen during the season we watched together, your beloved Steelers charged through the 2005 season, amazingly winning their final seven games before going all the way to win Super Bowl XL. You're both winners, Eddy, hard-working winners.

Teaching the Children

One April afternoon, a couple came in and browsed through the store, picking up figurines, statues, ornaments and books. Others came and left, until these two were the only ones in Angel Wings with me. As they approached the counter, Eric spoke.

"I don't know why we came in here, but if feels so comfortable," he said. "Again, I haven't a clue why, but I'm compelled to tell you about our son, Bobby." His wife, Stella, nodded with a gesture of reassurance.

After taking a long deep breath, Eric told me that they had a beautiful son named Bobby. He loved the little children and especially enjoyed romping with his little nieces and nephews, making them laugh. Twenty years ago, five months into his seventeenth year, Bobby started complaining of headaches. Eventually they became so severe that they set up a doctor's appointment for him. After some testing and a CAT scan, they learned that a tumor was growing inside Bobby's brain and he needed an operation immediately.

During his recovery from the operation, Bobby had a stroke and quit breathing. The doctors performed a tracheotomy and placed a respirator tube in his throat. Bobby's mother and father were in shock. Day and night, they stayed by his side. Two weeks went by with out any improvement. One night, his mother prayed and asked God to allow Bobby to open his eyes on her upcoming birthday.

On the day of Stella's birthday, Eric walked into the room first, as usual, and stood on Bobby's right side. Stella walked around to Bobby's left, opposite of her husband. No words were spoken. For the first time in more than two weeks, Bobby opened his eyes. He moved his head to his left and, as he looked directly into his mother's eyes, maneuvered his right arm from underneath the covers, pointed to her and mouthed "I love you." Then he fell back to sleep.

A short time later, Bobby's health began to deteriorate. Eric and Stella were advised to have the respirator removed so Bobby could slip away quietly and peacefully. It was an extremely tough decision for them to make, as it would be for any parent.

They made the decision to have the tube pulled on a Saturday and, after spending several hours with their son, left to go home for the night. That night, Bobby came to his mother in a dream. Stella was in awe at how well Bobby looked. He was aglow and his color was a radiant pink. In the dream, Bobby kneeled down next to his mother as she sat in her favorite chair and he told her that he loved her dearly. He asked her not to mourn for him, as he was going to a beautiful place and all was well. The next day, Bobby took his last earthly breath and passed into another place.

That wasn't the end of the story. As tears flowed down Stella's cheeks, Eric went on to say that a few months after his son's passing, Bobby began to visit his parents frequently. "

He doesn't come to us in dreams," Eric explained. "He visits with us just as we are doing right now. Bobby tells us that he is very busy where he is and that one of the things he does is teach children. He helps prepare the babies that are coming into this world." Although Stella was crying, both she and Eric knew that Bobby's life hadn't ended. He had important things to do and he was just where he needed to be, helping those who needed him.

CHAPTER SEVEN

Come, Sail Away

Still wiping the dream sleep from my eyes on a cool winter morning in the midst of the holiday season, I realized that another teacher had just entered my life, a woman I had never seen before. As I rolled out of bed, I was trying to understand the significance of the picture of the woman in the dream.

I stumbled along the side of the bed, walking toward the bathroom, when the big toe on my right foot made contact with the edge of the doorway. I heard a crack as a sensation of pain made its way from my brain down to my big toe. Then, as I bent over to hold my foot, my forehead slammed into the door frame, putting a crease in my forehead. Stunned and bouncing around the floor, I clutched my foot with both hands and let out some choice words more closely associated with soldiers, sailors, rap singers and bottom feeders, waking Pamela with all the commotion.

"What happened? What's wrong with you? Are you all right?"

I tried to walk upright on my own two feet, like any ordinary Homo sapiens. Still limping around the room, moaning and uttering expletives, I hastily told her, "It's okay, it's okay. I had a dream."

"You had a dream?" Confused by my answer and shaken by the sudden awakening, she then asked a question I was becoming accustomed to. "What's the matter with you?"

With pen in hand, a creased lump throbbing on my forehead and an enlarged big toe, I managed to grab the nearest piece of paper and write down what I had just seen in my dream, though I didn't understand it. A young, petite woman of stunning beauty with gorgeous strawberry-blond hair was sitting in an old, large, wooden wheelchair that had big wheels with hard rubber wrapped around the rigid metal connecting the dark wooden structure. The image I saw in the dream looked like a framed picture. Did the frame have a purpose? Was it a metaphor?

Inside the frame was a background of sky blue. The floor underneath the wheelchair was made of wooden slats, almost as if it were the deck of a ship. The woman wore a day dress with prints of lavenders and blues running through it. The dress, although pleasant, was out of place, out of time. It belonged on an older woman. The beautiful woman didn't say a word. She just sat in the chair and looked at me with penetrating eyes, as if she were looking through me. I felt as though she was hiding something from me—a secret from her past? Maybe it was something she felt was simply not relevant at this time.

Deep down in my gut, I knew there was a message for me in this dream. *You will not forget this. The meaning and memory will stay.* For the time being, I let go of my puzzling over it, put the pen down and got ready for work. Glancing in the mirror at the new growth on my forehead, I limped off to start my day with the phone company, grumbling underneath it all.

Later that afternoon, Lisa, the hospice volunteer coordinator, called. "Jerry, we have an elderly patient at the Park Regency in the East Valley and we thought of you for our new hospice patient. She is ninety-three years young, doesn't have any specific debilitating disease, but she is declining and, at times, combative."

"Combative. So you thought of me?" I asked.

Lisa giggled and said that she had met with the other coordinators and they thought I might be a good match because of my humor and patience. "If she doesn't like you, you'll know it right away. And you will be sent the usual info packet."

"Thanks, Lisa. And do you know that I can't wait for tomorrow?"

"And why is that, Jerry?"

"'Cuz you get better looking every day," I answered and hung up the phone.

The information packet arrived in the mail and as I reviewed it, I saw something that made my hair stand on end. The patient was in the fourth wing and in room 444. According to *The Messengers* by Julia Ingram and G. W. Hardin and *Healing with the Angels* by Dr. Doreen Virtue, the number 444 represents the power of God's love and indicates that angels are close right now.

Everything else I read looked quite ordinary for a hospice patient and, as usual, described her medical history, family structure and other details. Her chief problem: confusion and agitation. Her current medications: Ecotrin (aspirin), Senokot for bowels, Ambien for sleeping, and Cardizem for the heart. She was incontinent, both bowels and bladder. She did not know the people around her, where she was, the time of day, etc. "Well", I thought, "if my blood wasn't getting to where it needed to go, I'd be a little confused too!"

Edythe (or "Edie," as she was called) had come to the Park Regency nursing home in Chandler after a short stay at the Madison, an assisted-living group home in Mesa. As far as facilities for the aged go, the Madison was a very comfortable place to be. A few days after arriving there, though, she fell and broke her wrist. From then on, her health had deteriorated at a fast pace.

I phoned the nursing home and arranged for my first visit. Approaching the front door, I took a deep breath and walked in, looking for the front desk. "Aha," I said to myself. As usual, it was off to the side, this time on the left. Winding my way around the facilities, I found the fourth wing and ambled up to the doorway of room 444. The door was open, so I rapped on the frame and announced myself. As I stepped in, I saw my new patient sitting next to the bed in a wheelchair with its back against the wall. "Hi, Edie. I'm Jerry from hospice. How are you today?"

Not moving a muscle, not saying a word, she followed me with her eyes. I stood a few feet away from her, not wanting to frighten her by getting too close.

"Edie, I'm here just to visit with you, to see how things are going for you here and to find out if there is anything I can do to help you feel more comfortable."

No response. With her arms on the armrests of the chair, she sat upright and appeared alert. At least she was keeping her eyes focused on me. Suddenly I realized that not only was Edie sitting in a wheelchair, but she was also wearing a white housedress with lavenders and blues running through it. *Can this be the woman I saw in my dream?* Maybe, but some things didn't fit. Unlike the woman in my dream, Edie wasn't in her prime and her chair wasn't an antique. Although her physical features were similar to those of the woman in the dream, and both didn't speak, the woman in front of me was thin with light hair, more orange than any other color.

Noticing a framed collage of pictures on the wall in her room, I asked her if it was okay to look at them. Knowing she wasn't going to say anything, I strolled over to take a peak. As I looked at the pictures of her grandchildren and her grown children, I spotted old pictures of Edie and her husband. *Oh, my God. There she was in all her beauty, grace and charm. She was the same strawberry blond in the framed picture from my dream!*

I spun around to say something to Edie about the pictures and found her busy moving her feet and maneuvering her wheelchair so her back was facing me. It didn't bother me. I was rubbing my forearms, trying to lay down the hair that was standing on end. "Okay, Edie," I said. "I'll leave you alone now. Remember, my name is Jerry and I'll stop by tomorrow to visit. Bye-bye."

I left room 444 in the fourth wing in amazement, my head spinning with questions. Who can I tell about this? What does it mean? Where is this whole process going? How do I sort this out and where is it taking me? Why is this happening to me? Here we go again, a whole pant-load of questions, with no answers in sight.

The following day, I returned to room 444. Edie was once again sitting in the wheelchair next to her bed. I pulled up the only normal chair in the room (I call it the visitor's chair) and sat down. She looked the same as before, confused but alert. "Hi, Edie. It's me, Jerry. I was here yesterday. We talked and I looked at the pictures of your family on the wall."

No answer. This went on for a while. I talked, she didn't. Her eyes never left me, though. On the third visit, she still wouldn't talk. After running out of ideas, I walked over to her, put my hand on her right arm and said," Edie, I'm coming back tomorrow whether you like it or not. Can I bring you something? A chocolate malt perhaps?" She nodded yes. Aha, Houston. We made contact!

Over the course of the next several weeks, I fed her chocolate malts and she opened up—not a lot, but just enough for me to know there was life still inside that suit of skin and bones housing Edie's soul. It took a while to know Edie. She was a puzzle and I had to put the pieces together.

I learned that Edie had been born into a large and poor family in the little hamlet of Lake Stevens, just a few miles east of Everett, Washington. Her parents had separated when she was just a child. She felt the sting of coming from a divided home and vowed never to be poor again. Dreaming of a better life for herself, she worked her way through college and taught school, saving her money for adventure. When she had earned enough money, she left the tiny village of Lake Stevens to hop on a Matson ocean liner in 1930 and set sail for paradise, a small island in the middle of the Pacific Ocean—Oahu.

She taught the children aboard the liner, and the ship's captain was so impressed with her that he always asked Edie to dine with him for the evening meal. After arriving in the Hawaiian islands, she began teaching in Honolulu. She met and fell madly in love with a young and handsome West Point graduate named Joe Carroll. The young officer was infatuated with this young, vivacious, good-looking strawberry blond, and they soon began a new path together. They traveled the world over, drinking from the cup of life, loving each other and producing a family of children along the way. They were part of the generation that saved the world from tyranny and made the Western world shine with endless possibilities for those who would live after them.

Wherever her husband was stationed, Edie always made life worth living. So beautiful and light on her feet, she graced the dance floor with her elegance. She gathered the wives and lovers of the other officers and planned grand evenings of gaiety and laughter. Edie was in love with life and lived it to the fullest, sharing her joy with everyone around her.

I had been able to coax Edie into telling me about her life by leading with questions about her past, like "What was your father's name? When you were a child, what gave you the feeling of freedom? Where did you grow up?" She answered what she could. Edie couldn't or wouldn't recall her father's name, but she did tell me that swimming in Lake Stevens is where she felt alive, could enjoy herself and feel genuine happiness. Of all the countries she and Joe had lived in, she loved Germany the most. Collecting antiques had become a passion for her and Germany had what she was looking for.

Now, at ninety-three, Edie had essentially given up. Her will to live had died when her lifelong partner of sixty-two years passed away from Alzheimer's disease, just six months before she arrived at the Park Regency. It was never her intention to live alone without her colonel. She had lived her life with her prince and now that he was gone, she didn't want to be around anymore. She was ready to check out and move on to a better place—a kinder, gentler world reminiscent of the grace, dignity, grand elegance, ballroom dancing, festive parties and pomp and circumstance of the military balls she had so loved.

Twice while visiting Edie, something out of the ordinary took place. Once, as we conversed, she motioned with her right arm as if she was pushing someone back. Her eyebrows curled and she said to no one I could see, "Not now, Lolly, go away!" I asked her who that was and Edie responded, "My sister." It happened one other time. "No, not now, I'm not ready to go!" she said emphatically. I thought it was rather amusing. Here she was, finally trusting me enough to talk to me, and her sister wanted to get into the act.

When I later flipped through the information packet to read more of the doctor's findings on Edie's health, I saw that the doctors had found no traits of delirium or hallucinations. That backed up my suspicions that Edie was indeed conversing with her sister.

This is not an unusual scenario. I had heard many reports of hospice volunteers whose patients nearing death spoke with deceased loved ones, angels, Jesus or God. It appears that close family or friends that have passed on do come to those who are ready to make their transition from this world to the next. Not only that, but many hospice volunteers report that when they are with a patient who is passing on, they see the patient's soul leave the body. They say it looks like heat waves rising from the chest. Many people have seen bright lights appearing in the room at the time of someone's passing or have seen or felt angels at the bedside, including Archangel Michael standing at the foot of the bed. It's not delirium or hallucination. Yes, Martha, there is life after life.

Edythe Carroll became much more than just a hospice patient to me. She also became my friend. She loved the chocolate malts I brought her and she would talk of happier times and places she had been that pleased her most. The last time I saw Edie she seemed more tired than usual and a bit more agitated. Upon my arrival, she maneuvered her wheelchair toward a small closet.

"What are you doing, Edie?"

"I'm packing my bags!" she snapped in a tone that sounded like I should know what she was doing and why. It caught me off guard.

"Where are you going?"

Her tone changed. It was authoritative, yet without anger or frustration. "I'm going home. Help me pack my bags. I am leaving here and I want to go home, now."

One week later, with her loving family gathered around her bedside, Edie passed on to be with her colonel.

Thank you, Edie, for coming into my life. You taught me many loving things and reminded me to be humble and to appreciate life as it comes. You showed me that not all lives are open books; some are private. Some people choose to share their sadness and happy moments, while others choose to keep memories to themselves. You taught me that life is to be honored and that each individual life is a precious gift. My place is not to judge, only to help those who are lost find their own way along their paths. Each path is resplendent in its own way.

And that old antique wooden wheelchair that Edie was sitting in when I first met her in the dream—well, it would have been no different than any wheelchair used on the Matson ocean liner in 1930.

Caught Between Two Worlds

A young couple in their early twenties entered the store from Fifth Avenue and approached the counter as I was placing new angel pins on a rack.

"Are you Jerry?" the young lady asked. When I told her yes, she said, "My name is Sonia and this is my friend, Gary. We live in Glendale and drove over this morning. I got your name from a friend of a friend. They say you talk to the angels."

I glanced up at them over my reading glasses. Gary was wearing an off-white T-shirt, faded jeans and a faded cap. He had a week's growth of beard, light skin and dark, wide, almond-shaped eyes, the same shape depicted in many paintings of Archangel Michael. I placed the last of the pins on the rack, walked around the counter and asked, "How can I be of service?"

"Gary sees dead people," Sonia said without hesitating. "My friends said you could help him." I shook Gary's hand and Sonia's and sat down with them at the counter.

"I don't know what I can do, Gary, but I'm here to listen. When you say you see dead people, how do they appear to you?"

"They look real, just as real as me and you talking here, but they're dead and they ask me for help. Once when I was a kid growing up in Oklahoma, I saw a French soldier on a horse. It scared me. He was looking down at me with pleading eyes and an outstretched hand and he said, 'Help me.' I didn't know what to do. I tried telling my parents, but they thought I was crazy." Gary's eyes began to tear up but he bravely continued in a halting, sputtering voice.

"I had a good friend who was eighteen and his father owned a sporting goods store. I bought a shotgun from his dad and my friend wanted to borrow it one weekend. I felt uneasy about it, but I let him borrow it anyway. He wound up shooting himself in the face with it. He's been dead for years, but he still comes to me and asks for help and I don't know what to do or say. Stuff like that happens to me all the time."

"When these things happen and the ones who have passed come to you, do you see, feel and hear them all at once?" I asked.

"All the time," said Gary, readjusting his cap.

"Wow," I said. "But you didn't come in to tell me that. I get the feeling that you want to know why they come to you and how you can deal with this in a more positive way."

Gary nodded. "They come to me all the time," he repeated.

I asked if he had told anyone else of this besides his girlfriend. He paused and looked down, pulling on the bill of his cap. Then he looked up at me and said, "I tried to tell my best friend, but he thinks I'm crazy too."

"I understand," I said. "But you know you're not crazy, don't you? You are gifted. You were born knowing; you're what some people have called an 'Indigo.' In other words, you have trouble with absolute authority. Let me guess, standing in line is a real problem for you. You have almost always seen a better way of doing things. You have had some trouble with your parents. Older adults just drive you crazy because you don't have time for their silly games and stupid ideas. Am I right? That's just some of the traits Indigos have."

His eyes began to well up again, telling me I was right.

"No, Gary, you're not crazy. You are a royal child of God and everything is as it should be. You are just very sensitive. You can walk into a room and know immediately if there has been an argument or not. What you want to know from me is how to handle all of the stuff that's happening to you."

"Yeah. I have moved three times since I've lived here, twice to houses and one time to a condo. I'm in the condo now and that's a big problem. Sometimes I feel really, uh, really yucky," he said, pulling this time on the front of his shirt, "like there's gooey stuff going on there."

"Tell me what you have experienced in the condo."

"When I look at the fish tank, sometimes I see a set of red eyes on the other side of it, looking back at me. Another time, I was lying on the couch and I felt like there was a big argument going on between two people on both sides of me and that one of them grabbed me. It felt as if I was being pulled out of my body. You know what I mean? That kind of stuff happens there a lot. That happened at times in the houses I lived in, but not as often as in this condo and it wasn't nearly as angry or scary. I don't quite know how to explain it," he said, reaching for the right words.

"I think you are doing a fine job, Gary," I assured him. "In fact, I'm really proud of you. You have a lot of guts coming to a perfect stranger and telling your story of seeing spirits around you. You are doing great and everything is okay. You also want to know how to see this stuff and experience it without having to feel all the negativity."

He interrupted me. "That's it. It's like I take it all on and then I'm stuck with it. I don't want it. I don't know what to do. I'm, I'm tired of it. I want it to go away at times, yet I want to know why these people are coming to me. Why don't they go where they are supposed to go? I guess that's what I'm trying to say."

"First of all, about your sensitivity and the stuff you are feeling in the condo. You are picking up the negativity from the people who lived there before you."

"Oh my God, you are so right," he said. "That's what I've been thinking it is. The condo is almost unbearable for me."

"Now, there are mediums, like James Van Praagh," I said, "who talk about those who die and are afraid of going to the light. They are sometimes filled with so much fear and guilt that they just stay where they are. Some call it limbo and others call it purgatory. Regardless of the name of the place, these people are stuck where they are. The ones you see come to you because they know you have the gift of seeing and hearing them. They do not come to you to frighten you. They come to ask you to help them.

"You can best help them by assuring them that it's okay to go to the light. The light is about love, unconditional love. Tell them, Gary, that they will not be punished or harmed. They will go to a place of kindness, love and serenity. No harm will come to them. Just tell them to go."

"Boy, that really helps me, Jerry. That's just what I needed to hear."

"Just a couple more things for you, Gary. You receive messages from your angels when you take a shower. That's when you are at peace and you are fresh and ready for the day. They talk to you there. When you step out of the shower and dry off is when the trouble begins, because you don't follow their advice. They talk to you, you listen and then shrug it off because others have told you that you are crazy. Gary, you are perfect in the eyes of God."

"How do you know all this stuff about me?"

"Your angels told on you, and they told me something else too. You are supposed to write about this. You have to write it all down and soon it will be in book form."

He reached up and pulled on the front of his cap with both hands as Sonia gently caressed his arm as if to pacify him.

"I just wrote four chapters!" he said. "I don't know how you know so much about me. I guess you really do talk to angels."

"Gary, you can ask your angels to lighten your load by keeping away the negativity and all the guilt and fear from the ones you see. You take it all on and now you want to rid yourself of all the heaviness. I'm going to call on Michael archangel right now to place the white light of love around you, to keep all negativity and fear away: *The only emotion that can penetrate the bubble is love, both inwardly and outwardly. And so it is!*

"From now on, Gary, call upon Michael archangel any time you feel you need him and he will be there. He will bring a legion of his angels with him, as many angels as you want. That is what you are to do to keep from taking on all the painful emotions that are emitted from those kinds of spirits. That is what I have for you, Gary."

The young man's eyes teared up again as he stood up from the spiritual bar stool.

"You've done so much for me," he said. "I never had a chance to get to know my grandfather. He passed to the other side and I've been told he was very spiritual and enjoyed having me around when I was a baby. He died before I knew him. I want to connect with him and I feel I can now."

I extended my hand to him. He looked at it and then said, "May I give you a hug? You have really helped me, Jerry. I don't know what to say."

I received his hug, wished him well and asked him to stop back and let me know how he was doing. He said he would, and with new confidence in his step and understanding in his heart, he and Sonia walked out the door and onto the avenue, hand in hand.

CHAPTER EIGHT

The Angels Made Me Do It

After each of my visits with Edie, I would have to complete the paperwork, preparing one copy for the nursing staff and the other for the hospice nurse, and follow up with a voice message on the phone. One day as I made out the reports in the cafeteria at the Park Regency, I noticed a lonely looking woman sitting by herself at a table. Her teeth were long gone and she was chewing on her gums. She was plump, Afro-American and, I guessed, in her early eighties. She had an easygoing way about her, and her short hair—nicely combed, not particularly curly and with more than a hint of gray—still had life to it. I picked up my papers, walked over to her table and sat down across from her.

"Hey there, good looking, are ya behaving yourself today?" At first, her eyes were half shut peering down toward the empty table. She then looked up at me and laughed a nice, quiet laugh. I can still see her toothless smile and her chest bouncing up and down.

"Hello, my name is Lucille" was pinned on her dress near her right shoulder.

"How's the food today, Lucille?" I asked. She grinned and chuckled a little, then she mumbled something that made absolutely no sense at all. That was okay. If you've been married for any length of time, you've been told the same thing: "You make no sense."

As the days and weeks passed, Lucille and I became good friends. After my visits with Edie, I would go looking for Lucille. Sometimes I would find her sitting in her wheelchair in the hall-way. At other times, she would be in the cafeteria or activity room. The activity room is the place in nursing homes where not much is going on except the ever-present TV, where Vanna White can be seen moving from left to right, lighting up the vowels and consonants. Wherever Lucille was, she was always alone.

On one of our visits in the cafeteria, Lucille and I were hav-ing one of our classic conversations. She would talk, and I would smile and listen. Then I would speak and she would laugh. We made a good pair. One of the aides, large and in her mid-to-late thirties, was sitting on a windowsill about thirty feet behind Lucille, facing me. She looked our way, seeing me for the first time as I sat with Lucille and filled out my paperwork.

"You can't talk to Lucille. She's had a stroke and doesn't talk to anybody," she said in the voice of a dictator with a third-grade education. Apparently because Lucille couldn't *start* a conversa-tion with someone, the cafeteria aide thought she simply couldn't speak. Lucille looked up at me, gave me her beautiful toothless smile and giggled.

"Oh, really," I said. "Well, we're having a pretty good conversation right now, ma'am." The aide returned my look with one that would have made Osama Bin Laden have a sex change operation, then slowly lifted herself off the windowsill and waddled into the kitchen.

One Sunday afternoon, while I was finishing my paperwork and conversing with Lucille in the cafeteria, a guy in his early forties and a girl of about twelve walked by the table where we were sitting and stood behind me. I turned and looked up, then realized immediately that they belonged to Lucille. He must have been her son and the girl her granddaughter. Both had stern and somber looks on their faces. Her son was staring at me, so I pushed back my chair, stood and introduced myself to them. He was not very pleasant and I felt as welcome as a fart in an elevator.

I got up and moved to an empty round table in a corner of the cafeteria to finish my report. I could not help but glance over at Lucille's table. How sad. No one talked. The smile was gone from her face. Not only was no one smiling, but no one was talking. All three were looking down at nothing in front of them.

Watching that scene around Lucille's table made me angry. In my heart of hearts, I knew it was not for me to judge, yet I did just that. My ego jumped to the forefront and projected: What the hell kind of society do we live in that our elders have become a big pain in the ass? Well, aren't we something!

We *are* something. Each one of us is a unique individual who carries distinct gifts, different from everyone else's, and that's a good thing. When we affirm that goodness in others, no matter what age or condition they are in, we honor their gifts and their life. It didn't seem that Lucille's son or granddaughter knew how to do that, though I couldn't blame them. Coping skills—you either have them or you don't; you're either taught them or you're not.

When someone we love is stricken with a debilitating illness and outwardly becomes a totally different person, what do we do? Panic, cry, feel sorry for ourselves, become angry with everyone and give up? Or do we take the lemons handed to us in our life cycle and make lemonade? Each situation requires its own unique response. I suppose there is no absolute right way to cope. We can only do the best we can with what we have.

And that's where the angels come in.

God gave us angels so we wouldn't be alone and to help us when we feel confused. They will help us in every situation we find ourselves in. All we have to do is call upon them and they will intervene on our behalf in ways we can't even imagine. Not only that, they nudge us (and at times knock us) in the right direction, sometimes to meet our own need, sometimes to meet another's need, and sometimes both.

Was it just a coincidence that Lucille happened to be in the cafeteria when I was looking for a quiet place to fill out my hospice paperwork? Not likely. In fact, I could have sat at any of the tables. There were always more chairs than people in that big hall. No, the angels made me do it.

There are a million Lucilles in homes, hospitals and nursing facilities everywhere. They are just sitting there alone, waiting for time to pass by, because time is all they have. The ego tells us to stay away from the unfortunate ones, stay away from uncertainty, avoid uncomfortable people, places and situations. Since the angels are an extension of God's love here on earth, it's their job to point us in the direction of those who could use a little tenderness, those who are capable of feeling and who need to feel love, joy and happiness, even if it's only for a few fleeting moments. You would be surprised at how magical a gentle touch of a warm hand or a pleasant smile from one to another can be.

While the Lucilles of the world have only time to contend with, we, on the other hand, have cluttered busyness. If we can free ourselves, even briefly, from our own self-made busyness, go to a place where a Lucille resides and spend some time with him or her, we will be rewarded in ways we least expect. *Go ahead and do it; it's what God wants you to do*—that's what the angels say.

I love you, Lucille. I know that your soul will find its way home and find the solace it craves. Within my memory, you will always be joyful, playful and chock full of life. Thank you for teaching me the value of seeing the glass as half full and not half empty. You will remain with me forever. And thank you, hospice, for the special care you give those in need. No one has to die alone in a darkened room anymore. If it hadn't been for a program like hospice, I wouldn't have had the chance to meet lovely Lucille at that lonely looking table.

Say It Loud, Say It Often

Marianne strolled lightly into the store and came to the counter, announcing that she had come to pay in advance for a class we were putting on. She said she was interested in a reading because she seemed to be at a plateau and was looking for direction. Marianne also went on to share a dream she had two weeks earlier.

"I was lying in a bed with many friends, looking up at the blue sky," she said. "A wispy white cloud appeared in the sky and it began to flutter. The cloud descended ever so lightly and began to take the shape of angel wings. As it got closer, I could see that the wings belonged to an angel. The angel came gently to me and said, 'I am here whenever you need me.' "

"Marianne, did she have a name and could you describe her?" I asked.

"Yes, she said her name was Della and she had a peaceful and loving face."

"Did you know the people you were with when the angel appeared?"

"That's the funny part," she said. "I knew them, but not from this lifetime. I mean, none of them were people I knew in my day-to-day life."

"Did you tell anyone about your dream?"

"Yes, I did. I told my mother and sister, and they thanked me for sharing it with them."

In my heart, I let out a loud *"Way to go!"* for Marianne. We don't have to be silent about our experiences with the Spirit world any longer. We needn't keep them a secret.

For all of you who have had, or are yet to have, encounters with angels or the Spirit world, I say: The world is hungering for truth, the higher truth. Say it loud, say it often. Welcome home.

CHAPTER NINE

The Lady in Lavender

"Uh, Pam...I had another one of those dreams."

"Oh," she said, letting the word linger. "Now what?"

Pam was busy packing our suitcases in the early hours of the morning. It was just three weeks after 9/11. We were going to Hawaii and trying not to think about the flight.

"No, no. It's okay," I assured her. I wanted to describe the dream to her to help me remember what the dream was about and so I could help her understand that something strange was going on in my world. "It's just that today we will see a lady wearing purple and lavender. She has a pile of brown hair tucked up under a big, wide-brimmed, light-brownish straw hat and she's in a wheelchair. As I saw it in my dream, we will see her coming into view from behind me on the left and she will pass to the right and out of view."

"Well, who is she and why is she coming into our lives?" Pam asked.

"You know, I don't know the answer to that."

I started scrawling the details of the dream on a notepad I keep by the bed in case I wake up remembering a dream about something or somebody. It had been two and a half years since I'd begun having dreams about people I hadn't yet met, and this was the third one.

"I'm getting that this dream is not for me as much as it is a confirmation for you," I said. "It's as if the angels are saying that it's time to include Pamela in these things."

Pam was starting to lose patience with me. "That's nice," she said hurriedly. "Now, get ready so the taxi driver doesn't have to blow his horn for us more than once."

"Yes, dear," I mumbled under my breath in a mild attempt to keep her from getting riled up. I always get the last word in, even if it's just "yes, dear."

"Hey, where's the camera?" I blurted out, suddenly concentrating on the day's activities.

"It's right where you left it last night, on the charger in the kitchen!" I wasn't being too successful at keeping Pam in a peaceful place.

I had just purchased a movie camera to take on our vacation to Maui and Oahu so I could video everyone at the gate as we waited to board the plane in case we crashed. I thought that if that happened, maybe the camera would be found intact and it could be analyzed and used as evidence. Because the entire boarding area would be on tape, the authorities could watch the video and be able to identify the bad guys. Then I would posthumously be given the keys to the city, and the mayor of Phoenix in an election speech would hold me up as a hero for having saved Phoenix from certain disaster.

We soon found ourselves waiting for our flight to Maui at Sky Harbor Airport in Phoenix. We arrived by 3:30 a.m., two and a half hours before our scheduled 6 a.m. departure, per the new security measures. We wandered around the terminal, half awake, half in a daze, until a coffee kiosk finally opened at 5 a.m. I shuffled over to it as I wiped the sleep from my eyes to focus on the task at hand: caffeine.

We sat at the only empty table, next to the walkway that runs up and down the terminal. I kept an eye on our gate while Pamela sat facing me, peering over my shoulder down the corridor where everyone walks from the main entrance to various destinations.

Drinking her glass of milk and eating a bagel, Pamela was enjoying the diversion of watching other people's journeys unfold, while I attempted to drink a scalding, strong cup of coffee and eat my sweet roll. To help cool my burning lips and scorched tongue, I carefully gripped the caramel pecan sweet roll to take a bite out of it, when Pam swallowed hard and gasped aloud, *"Is that her?"*

I turned to my left and looked over my shoulder to see what Pamela's eyes were fixed on—-a woman in purple pants and a lavender floral blouse wearing a big, wide-brimmed light-brownish straw hat. Someone was pushing her down the long corridor in a wheelchair. It was the woman in my dream alright. The questions formed quickly in my mind: Why is this happening? Does she play a significant role in my life? In Pam's life? Do we enter her life? And what is it with all that lavender anyway? Am I supposed to do anything beyond noticing her and wondering about color schemes?

Loads of questions, no answers. We watched the woman disappear into the crowd at the gate, pondering the magic we had just experienced as we finished our breakfast. We were both bemused and confused at the sight of the woman from my dream. More questions flew into my gray matter: How do I approach her? Do I tell her of the dream? I knew I had to talk to her, but how? When? We left the kiosk, hoping that God would sort it out and get back to us with the answers.

We arrived at our gate to find the area packed with people. We spotted two vacant seats near the big windows along the back wall, sat down and set our carry-ons next to us.

"Look over to your right," Pamela said quietly yet excitedly.

There she was, wheelchair and all, alongside the man who was assisting her, her husband I presumed. Should I say something? Right, like I was going to walk over to her and say, "Hi, nice lady. You look very pleasant this morning with your purples, lavenders and big straw hat. Oh, by the way, you were in my dream this morning. Do you happen to know why?"

I imagined myself being dragged away by security guards and interrogated, sitting on a cold steel chair in a dark, barren room with a light bulb dangling from the ceiling, inches from my head. Meanwhile, my wife would be long gone. I would later find her being serenaded by young Hawaiian kanes in grassy skirts on the beach in Maui. The young men would be offering her drinks with umbrellas, doing the hula, and gracing her with fruits and freshly caught fish served on a silver platter.

I forced my mind away from that scenario and focused my attention on the matter at hand. As planned, I pulled out my video camera, documenting everyone in the boarding area. You know, just in case.

We landed on the beautiful island of Maui and felt the serenity of paradise. From there, we flew to Honolulu to spend a few aloha, laid-back, sun-filled days on Waikiki Beach before returning to Lahaina, Maui, where we had dreamed of opening some kind of a shop some day. With just two days left in island paradise, Pamela and I lounged in a little courtyard off Front Street, lined with shops and boutiques. The banyan tree in the middle of the courtyard gave shaded shelter to the shoppers. Taking a break from our souvenir hunt, dreaming about a place on the Islands where we could launch our dream, we sat savoring our chocolate ice cream cones.

As the melting ice cream continued to drip from my lower lip, we both spotted the lavender lady again. She was sitting at one of the patio tables in the courtyard along with her husband, sipping a soft drink with a wedge of sliced pineapple perched on the rim of her glass. They seemed quite content with each other, gazing about the immediate surroundings.

I wiped the ice cream from my chin, knowing that I had to tell her that I had seen her in a dream the morning of our flight to Hawaii. I was convinced that, like the others I had seen in my dreams, she too was a teacher and I was supposed to learn something from her. This was my chance and I didn't want to let it pass by. I needed to hear what she had to say. Pamela and I nodded in agreement and we walked over to her table.

We introduced ourselves and made small talk. They began the conversation by saying that they had stayed at a time share on the Big Island the entire time, relaxing and basking in the warm sun, feeling the gentle breezes caress their bodies and taking in the breathtaking sunsets. You could tell by their peaceful and laid-back attitudes that they had found the aloha spirit of

Hawaii and were more than happy to share it.

Then it was my turn. I began to tell the story of my dream. Both the woman and her companion sat relaxed and listened politely. When I finished, she looked straight ahead toward the banyan tree, paused and said, "I believe in angels too."

Had I mentioned angels? I was sure I hadn't. I'd simply told her that I'd seen her in a dream a couple of hours before spotting her at the airport. So both Pamela and I were a bit bewildered when she mentioned believing in angels.

That was basically all there was to our encounter with the lady in lavender and her husband. They were certainly nice people, but I expected more information. We had shared our experiences and the beauty we had found in the Hawaiian Islands. We wished them well and they wished us well. Pamela and I excused ourselves and walked out of the courtyard and onto the tiny, busy main street of Lahaina.

What was this encounter about? We didn't know, but we were sure there was something more to this than we were consciously aware of, maybe something about angels that would play out later in our lives. For now, the prophetic dream and the encounter in the courtyard was yet another puzzle with a large piece missing.

A Salute from Feathered Friends

Across the street and a few storefronts down from Angel Wings, a gentleman, formerly of Iran, owns a little Native American gift store that caters mostly to the tourists walking along the avenue. During the quiet times, he likes to sit on a chair just outside the door and feed the pigeons. I guess that's why they never come to my side of the street.

March is one of the busiest months of the year and many people walk the avenue and drivers search for a coveted parking space. I walked to the front of my store one March afternoon and noticed a bird in the middle of the street flapping its wings, trying to right itself and stand. It could not. Immediately, I knew its back was broken.

A man and woman were making their way across the street. Noticing the nearly mortally injured pigeon, the man lifted his foot and not so gently nudged the bird toward the curb. It was still desperately fluttering and flapping its wings, trying in vain just to stand.

Instinct took over and I quickly went into the back room, dug out a little cardboard box and walked outside to retrieve the pigeon. I gently lifted her broken body, which was warm and soft, placed her in the box and walked her back to an area protected from all activity. She was dying, and I placed her down so she could have some peace in her last few minutes of life.

A little over an hour had lapsed and I glanced at the clock on the wall. It was 4:44 p.m. and I chuckled as I thought of Nick Bunick's 444 experiences. When the angels were intervening in his life, he would be awakened at exactly 4:44 a.m. and so would his business partners. He says that 444 means that angels are near.

I walked to the front of the store to take a look outside and could not believe my eyes. Lined up like soldiers on the sidewalk were nine pigeons in a V formation, all facing the door of the store. I felt goose bumps all over. I had never before had any pigeons near my store, nor have they ever returned. I believe it was a salute, their way of thanking me for caring for one of their own during her time of need. I felt humbled.

After closing the store that day, I placed the pigeon in its final resting place, a hole I had dug by an old eucalyptus tree near the courtyard. I thanked God for the experience, which had validated the need we all have to reach out and follow our instincts. I learned once again that merely listening to the constant murmurs of our heart can be the beginning of change and healing as we consciously move away from our chosen self-alienation and make the choice for unity, affinity and participation in co-creating reality.

CHAPTER TEN

Talk to Me

It was the winter of my discontent. I found myself at a corner of Crossroads Drive in the middle of a desert with a racing
mind. With nearly twenty-nine years under my belt with the
phone company, I was hoping to reach the milestone of thirty
years of service before immersing myself in something totally
different. But with everything that had gone on in my life
recently, I was getting impatient. Could I complete my thirty
years? Did I want to?

My dream teacher Eddy Cooper, the private Edythe Carroll,
the beautiful Lucille and the lady in lavender were permanently
ingrained in my swirling mind. God got an earful from me every
day, hearing from me morning, afternoon and even nightly. I
had a hard time sleeping and I couldn't stop praying. Mostly, I
posed questions and prayed for guidance, saying: "What do I do
next?" "Help me with the next step, please," and "Thank you for
prayers answered."

Pamela and I had been thinking about what our next steps

could be. We had toyed with the idea of opening our own store for several years, and quite by accident we found out that the artwork of two artists Pamela liked were being offered in galleries that could be bought as franchises. The style of the two painters was very different. One called himself a painter of light and the other did whimsical and gentle paintings of children. Both had a large following of dedicated buyers. When we found out that anybody could own a franchise, even us, I thought, "Well, there you go—a nice way out of the phone company and into something that brings joy into people's lives. What better way to live than to bring happiness to others and be content doing it."

Through all the years that we had considered owning our own store, only one thing had kept us from doing so: we lacked guts. We had a fear of the unknown, of doing something by ourselves without a road map, so it just never happened. We began having children along the way in our married life and security was the top consideration in picking our jobs. So we stayed in our secure jobs, paying the bills, chasing the kids around, and all the while dreaming about having our own business one day.

After checking out the websites of the two artists and the gallery information, we decided to seriously look into opening a gallery. If the first opportunity didn't pan out, we could always go with plan number two, the other artist. I sent sixteen hundred dollars to the first artist's gallery franchise company and then spent six days at a hotel I paid for to attend the artist's six-day "university."

While at the university, I became concerned about three things. First, the five people who manned the front office were all from different ethnic backgrounds, showing a seemingly diverse and progressive company. Yet there was something about it that put me on the alert, although I couldn't put my finger on it.

Second, midway through the week of classes, we were bussed to a nearby town to visit the factory where the paintings were placed on canvas. We were told not to call it a factory. I noticed something at the facility that was quite different from the front office. All the people working on the assembly line, constructing the frames and applying the pictures to canvas, were Hispanic, every single one of them. Most did not speak English. I know because I stepped away from our group and talked with some of the employees on the assembly line. In contrast, every one of the managers was an Anglo. When I questioned what we were seeing, a couple in our group chastised me. Nevertheless, a bell was starting to sound inside my head, one that rang like a school bell signaling the end of a session.

My third concern surfaced when I went to my interview with the vice president of the company on the last day of school. Everyone was called into his office for an interview according to how much money each member of the class was willing to pour into franchises. Each of my classmates had already had an interview with him and I was the last one called into his office. The company wanted each person to ultimately own three galleries. I had enough for one gallery.

The vice president's secretary opened up the door and motioned for me to enter. I sat across the big cherry wood desk in a little vinyl chair. He was wearing a three-piece business suit. He perched himself toward the edge of his huge, overstuffed brown leather chair, his forearms leaning on the edge of his desk with his hands folded tight. The "interview" was going well, I thought, but all he wanted to do was talk. So I listened.

Finally, he asked me if I had any questions. "Yes, I have one question. What does your company do for the community in which it resides?" I asked with a concerned tone. He moved slowly away from his desk and slid back into the overstuffed leather chair. The leather made popping sounds as he pushed himself back. As he sank farther back into his chair, the popping turned to a slow groaning sound. He sat silent for what seemed an eternity to me. He turned his eyes away from me and looked toward the front window of his office and then back to me.

He said that the artist did sketches at the grand openings of his galleries. "So, the franchisee can have an auction and donate the money raised from the sketch to charity," he said.

The school bell was ringing louder and louder. It felt as if my head was about to explode. I took a deep breath, stood up, shook his hand and made an about face as I said goodbye to door number one. As the boys in the 'hood would say, "I got schooled!" I chalked up the experience as another lesson in the value system of retail marketing.

With door number one closed, we decided to look into purchasing a gallery for the painter of children. I had been playing phone tag with the business manager for those galleries, Bob, trying to check on details and ask the many questions associated with starting a business, including seeking his guidance on the proper location for us to open a gallery. He seemed elusive at times, but I kept on him with dogged determination. Things had to be crystal clear for me and some of the wording that Bob was using in our conversations seemed a bit cloudy.

Then, seemingly out of the blue, word was going around the phone company that Salt Lake City was looking for volunteers.

Ah yes, I know what volunteering is, but what did the phone company mean by it? They were looking for phone technicians who would like to travel to Salt Lake to work the Olympic venues. We would get the same pay as well as an allowance for food since we had to stay in small hotels. The company would fly us home for Thanksgiving and Christmas. Wow, I thought, wouldn't that be something to work the Olympics! I jumped at the chance. Where would my volunteering lead me this time?

I planned on bringing two items with me to Salt Lake City to keep my spirits up and to help me find the right path after my time with the phone company was over. One was a deck of oracle cards. When I have a question or need, I get myself in a quiet place and meditate to remove the chatter of my mind before asking a question. I then shuffle the deck of cards until they get clumpy and stick together. I set them down, pick the number of cards that feels right to me and then turn them over one at a time. Each card conveys a specific meaning, a meaning that may be different for each person.

For instance, if I turn over a card that says "study," I may interpret that to mean that before I jump into anything, I should look at all aspects of what I want to do. If a card reads "ideas and inspiration," it may tell me that the universe likes my ideas and is guiding my inspiration. If the next card says "divine timing," it could be letting me know that my time and God's time are in sync and that the time for action is now. This is all done intuitively and I loved it. The second tool I brought with me was a new book designed to help those who needed direction in their lives. Direction is exactly what I needed—along with a map, a compass and someone or something to tell me how to make use of them all.

That something was starting to appear in the form of my newfound friend, meditation. I began meditating in the mornings and then just before going to sleep. While in meditation in the mornings, I had recently begun getting intuitive hits that turned out to be correct. At first, I was amazed; then it began to be fun—and it still is.

In my meditations, for instance, I would visualize a white light encompassing my work vehicle to keep me safe as I drove to my work locations. The next day, I would look into my rearview mirror and find no one tailgating me, plenty of room between me and the vehicle in front of me, and no problems from drivers in the adjoining lanes of traffic. It felt great and I thanked the Great Spirit for the protection I had asked for.

At times during my meditations I would ask for guidance, and I was starting to get direct answers. Not only could I hear the words, but I could feel each word deep down in the core of my being: *You must do it now. The world needs compassion, love, peace, hope and serenity now more than ever. It is what you want, and it is what God wants you to do.*

I still didn't know exactly *how* I was going to provide all those things to the world, or even to me for that matter. Was it through opening a gallery? If so, it had to be with the second painter since the first door of opportunity had slammed shut like a thick metal door at the end of a long corridor, echoing from one end to the other and back again. Yet somewhere way down inside of me, I kept thinking about a "store." I shrugged it off as an idea that was coming from my own mind because Pamela and I had years ago talked of having a store of our own.

The world needs compassion, love, peace, hope and serenity now more than ever. Those words kept floating around in my head. "Okay, God, talk to me," I said. "If it's supposed to happen 'now,' then why aren't my next steps clear?" I wanted answers and a timetable, but no answers came. I lamented to Pam that if only the phone company would offer an incentive for leaving the company early, it might be easier to get going with this "plan."

"Companies do that for their employees every once in a while, Gerald," Pamela said.

"Yeah, well, not this company. They'd rather have us drop dead and then argue about whether or not to pay the death benefits," I snarled.

"Now, now, you've got to think positive."

"I am. I'm positive that that's how they think!"

"But that's not what you've been learning lately, and you know it."

"You're right. Everything is done in God's time. I just wish God and I could synchronize our watches. The not knowing is driving me crazy!"

"Oh, you've been there before," she murmured.

"Hey, I heard that!"

"Well, try and stay positive, Gerald! You just have to put it in God's hands, that's all," Pamela pleaded.

"Yes, dear."

I surrendered, for the moment anyway. It took me a little while, but I was learning that our time and God's time are in different zones. Things don't happen in Eastern, Central, Mountain or Pacific time, or in any of the time zones of earth. Everything happens in God time.

On a warm sunny day in late September, Pamela helped

pack my bags for Salt Lake City. It was a bittersweet time. Going someplace different and working on something new for the first time is a real rush for me, but leaving Pamela behind for months pulled on my heartstrings. With the three children in college and me in Utah, I didn't know how she would take it. Pam was all for it, though.

As I was sitting on the plane, waiting for it to take off, I reached into the carry-on bag, pulled out the oracle cards and slowly shuffled them to see if there were any messages about the pilot or co-pilot in the cockpit. Until then, I had only used the oracle cards to do readings for myself, but I was curious about what was on the mind of the pilot. What have I got to lose, I thought. If it works on me, it will work on anyone. After shuffling the cards, I laid them down on the little tray in front of me. But I got a feeling, an intuitive hit, as I call it, that the pilots were busy and their angels didn't want any interference. So I didn't read the cards. There are ethics, you know, and privacy is just one of them.

Later I got another intuitive hit along with a visual in my third-eye charka, the energy center that is above the bridge of the nose between the eyebrows, the place where we can "see" with our inner sight. I asked a flight attendant if one of the pilots was contemplating retirement in the near future. She never got back to me about it.

As we exited single file after landing in Salt Lake City, both pilot and co-pilot were emerging from the cockpit. I heard a voice from within saying, *"Speak your truth lovingly."* I obeyed. I spoke to the first pilot who came through the cockpit door. "Something tells me you've had your eyes on a piece of country property with tall pine trees and a log cabin in high country near mountains. Go ahead, it's time," I said. "God wants you to." The pilot's jaw all but hit the floor. I ducked my head, left the plane and melted into the airport crowd.

After checking into my new abode, a two-story hotel with a small unheated outdoor pool on the outskirts of Salt Lake City, I phoned Pamela to let her know I had arrived safely. "It's not too bad," I said. "There's a kitchenette here, so I can save some cash by cooking myself, plus there are two Bibles in the room."

"Why two Bibles?" she asked.

"One for Christians and one for Mormons, I guess. I'll let you know as soon as I can about what Olympic venue I've been chosen for."

In the application for volunteers that I had filled out in Mesa, we were asked which venues we wanted to work at, such as the ice-skating competition, the basketball arena, the ski jumping competition, etc. I had chosen bobsledding and luge. Management said we could rate our picks in order of their importance to us and that those of us with more seniority were more likely to get what we had asked for. It felt so exciting. What a way to end my career with the phone company. I had gone from working on the old single-line wire, climbing and removing poles that had stamps on them dating back to 1909, to placing fiber-optic cable. To end my career at the Olympics would be like icing on the cake. I couldn't wait to get there.

Early the next morning after leaving my room, I walked down the narrow hallway into the lobby by the front desk. Just for the record, the front desk was on the right. Other technicians who had volunteered to work there were standing around the coffee pots and donuts—guys and gals from Iowa, Washington, Oregon, New Mexico, Colorado, the Dakotas, Minnesota,

Wyoming, Montana, Idaho and Arizona. I grabbed a cup of java as we waited for rides to designated areas surrounding the city.

As I breathed in the aroma of overly strong coffee, I heard a rumor buzzing around that some of us weren't going to be anywhere near the Olympic village as promised. I didn't pay much attention. I was more eager to meet my new crew and manager and to see the beautiful vistas surrounding the picturesque Salt Lake City, and I was thinking about connecting with Bob about possible gallery locations and start-up costs.

The orientation started and I found myself sitting at an oval table with twenty-four other newbies, receiving maps and telephone numbers for various help desks, managers and local technicians. Part way through the orientation, one of the managers in the room handed me a fax, saying it had come last night and I was to call about it as soon as possible.

I was confused. If it was so important for me to call ASAP, why was I being handed the fax an hour into the orientation?

I quickly read the fax, which was from my manager in Mesa, and got quite a surprise. My request to the universe had been granted. The fax said, in part, that the phone company was now offering early retirements with a possible bonus. As soon as the meeting ended, I called my manager. As usual, the first-line managers had no information for us other than a phone number for the personnel department at the headquarters in Denver. When I called there, they didn't have any information either. Great, I thought. Here we go again—the company is offering something, you call about it and they haven't heard of it. Corporate America. Sometimes I think they own stock in pharmaceuticals; they put their workers through so much unneeded stress that the workers need medication.

Later that night, the unexpected news turned my mind into a squirrel cage. It seemed as if there were two squirrels up there chasing each other, running around and around trying to find a way out. They couldn't. Then my head turned into a committee room, with all the parts of me talking at the same time. "This should be done." "That should be done" "Why not quit now?" "Get all your ducks in a row." "You have to work things out with Bob right away. He'll find a great location for your gallery." "Stay positive." "What about Bob? Something is amiss—he's not telling me everything I need to know." "Why wait—panic now." It went on and on and on.

I turned to the book I had brought along, *Your Heart's Desire* by Sonia Choquette. I thumbed through it, then put it back on the desk. Her book was a guide to helping people find their hearts' desires and act on them. Sonia had come to Scottsdale the weekend immediately following the 9/11 tragedy to conduct a workshop. "The lady's got guts," I had thought, "flying from Chicago to Phoenix on the heels of that attack." I went to hear her message and purchased a copy of her book. The timing of the workshop seemed to have been divine as far as I was concerned.

Doreen Virtue's *Healing with the Angels* oracle cards were sitting on the coffee table. Before I began shuffling, I meditated on God's loving angels and visualized the winged ones carrying me through the heavens and away from any fears I might have. A silver-white cloud of peaceful calm enveloped me. Minutes later, my mind began to clear. I shuffled the cards and placed five of them down, one at a time. I put down the remainder of the deck, looked at the cards laid out before me and gave myself a reading.

It was one of the strangest readings I had yet experienced, a message that was both audible and visual. I could hear the words from just outside my head and feel them inside too, close to each ear: *Two doors will close and a third will open. Walk through it with faith.* Along with this message, I received a visual in my third-eye chakra. It was like a movie in slow motion that was slightly tilted in another dimension, like the early *Twilight Zone* TV shows. Through my third eye, I could see an arm extending to the doorknob of the first and then the second door, one at a time. The first and second doors appeared to be made of a solid dark wood. The arm in the vision grabbed the doorknobs and pulled them shut.

The third door looked somewhat smaller than the first two, almost like a window, and it was ajar. The door was also a different color and texture (it seemed brighter and golden) and the doorknob was intensely inviting. Slowly, the door opened. As my eyes gazed upon the third door, a voice said to me: *"Walk through it with faith."*

I didn't think too much about this vision, except that it seemed both real and surreal at the same time. Before going to bed, I called Pam, told her about the reading and kept her abreast of recent events. The conversation was filled with excitement and fear, fear of the unknown. Like me, she was both excited and leery of what the future might bring, yet we both knew that our prayers were being answered.

The next day, management had us all sit around a big oval table for a teleconference. It was there that we learned that the company had made the exciting decision to offer an early retirement to those who wanted it and a small incentive to boot. I was ecstatic. It was just the little nudge I had been praying for! I would now have a chance to do something with the art gallery. I gladly filled out the paperwork for retirement with one condition. I would agree to retire as long as I could fulfill my side of the volunteer agreement in Salt Lake City. To my surprise, after some wrangling, management agreed.

With these new developments, Pamela and I decided that I should contact Bob right away to let him know that we would soon be ready to open our gallery. We didn't even care a lot about the location, as long as it was profitable and not in cold country. I called Bob and left a message. I also called the artist's studio, where they told me that Bob was in the process of moving and that they would let him know I was trying to reach him.

In the meantime, I tried to stay focused on the work at hand, which didn't go exactly as planned. The clowns had lured us to Salt Lake City under false pretenses. As it turned out, only a handful of techs outside of Utah were assigned to the venues high in the mountains near the Olympic village by Park City. The rest of us, and there were hundreds, simply backfilled for the technicians in and around Salt Lake City. We had been given the shaft. We shouldn't have been surprised, I guess. At least it would be one of the last lies I would ever be told by the company I had worked with for years. Are there corporate leaders out there willing to stand on their own two feet and tell the truth? It seems to me that that would be easier than standing on their corporate heads and telling a lie, but maybe that's just me.

At least I was assigned to the suburbs and outlying areas. I liked that much better than being stuck working in the city proper—more windshield time. I drove every morning from the little hotel the company had put me in to the northern suburbs. Every day I would glance toward the mountainside of the city to view the grandeur of the Mormon Temple. Quite a site in the evening, too, all lit up. It looked to me like an American version of the Vatican.

Anxious to get things moving, I called Bob and left another message. I called again and again. Days of unreturned phone calls went by and a knot was forming in my stomach. Finally, one Monday morning after weeks of silence, I couldn't stand it any longer. The thoughts of retiring, the unanswered phone calls and being on the road and away from my family for months were draining me. Tension had been slowly building deep down inside and it was ready to explode. While driving Interstate 15 on my way to work through the city, my heart was pounding against my chest. I glanced to my left, saw the Mormon Temple and blew up. With both hands gripping the steering wheel as tightly as I could, I yelled at the top of my lungs.

"*Okay,* God, *what the $#%* is going on?*" I kept at it, ranting and raving and driving down the highway.

"Why doesn't this clown call?" I yelled. "I put my retirement papers in, I've done all this footwork and I get no answers! No affirmations from you! Nothing! All I get is silence! One door has already been closed. Please, God, give me an answer, a sign, anything, but I need it now! Is going with this art gallery the right move? Talk to me, God! *Talk to me!*"

Still clutching the steering wheel at the old ten o'clock and two o'clock position, face beet red and veins bulging out of my neck so hard that they were throbbing, I heard the cell phone ring. I was taking deep breaths to calm myself and to keep the truck in one lane. "Hello," I said in between breaths, "this is Jerry speaking."

There was a long pause before I heard a voice. It was Bob. I took a deep breath and said, "Bob, I've been waiting to hear back from you. I put in my retirement papers and my wife and I are eager to join your team."

Again, a long pause and then he spoke.

"Well, Mr. Van Slyke, I called to let you know that we have decided to take the artwork of our artist into a new venue."

My jaw dropped. "What do you mean?"

"Mr. Van—"

"Call me Jerry, Bob." This didn't sound good.

"Jerry, we've decided to take her work to the homes of prospective buyers and introduce the product in a party atmosphere."

"What about the galleries?" I asked, confused.

Bob continued in his monotone voice, "We are going to grandfather the galleries that are already in existence and concentrate on the home market, and those with the galleries will be able to tap both markets."

Seeing in my mind a dark hole extending itself deep into a black abyss, I realized once again that I had been given the shaft. It seemed as if a game was being played out before me, but I didn't remember putting on a uniform and volunteering to join in. I pressed "end" on the face of the cell phone, stopping the conversation with Bob. Door number two had just been slammed in my face like a hockey puck from a slap shot.

So there I was, driving along a highway in Utah on my way to work, ready to retire with no place to go. Six tiny words entered into the gray matter between my ears: What do I tell my wife?

"Oh my God!" said Pam when we spoke that evening.

"Well, oh my God is right," I blurted. "At least God answered my prayers! I needed an answer and I simply couldn't wait any longer."

Pamela paused and her voice softened. "Do you remember the messages you told me you received from that reading you gave yourself?"

"Oh, God! I do." The image of the third door and the message came before me again: *Two doors will close and a third will open. Walk through it with faith.*

Interesting concept, this idea of faith, the word so often used yet rarely followed. I knew little about business (and so far I've kept it that way), but I did know that before jumping into something like owning your own business, there are certain factors to consider, like demographics as well as attaining business and financial advisors and possibly a backer to help insure a solid investment opportunity. I mean, you don't just get your savings out of the bank, throw the money to the wind and say, "I believe in you, God. I trust the faith I have in you and your plan for me." But that's what I did. When the stock market took a wild dive into a black abyss from mid-1999 and well into the year 2000, it took most of my life savings from the phone company with it. What little I had left went into my new venture.

February 1 of that year was my last day with the telephone company. Many of the technicians had been sent home from Utah early, me included. So much for deals. On the day they told me I would be going home, I quit. After nearly thirty years, I quit.

It was a strange feeling to walk away from something you had known and had done for such a long time, but I did it. I quit when there were still bills to pay, including the mortgage, multiple car payments, insurance, utilities, and everything else that is a part of life. I quit with no place to go and with all my careful plans in shreds. There's an old saying that I was beginning to believe: "We plan. God laughs." After watching me, I thought, God's stomach must ache something fierce. But as it turned out, if God was laughing, it was in anticipation of what was yet to come.

Call My Name

One day, a widow in her seventies bounded through the front door of Angel Wings. Her name was Merrill, and her hands and feet were wracked with arthritis. The joints were so swollen that it was difficult for me not to look at them. Yet Merrill was full of pep, full of life and did not complain about her situation. She was quite chatty and to the point.

"I'm looking for Michael archangel. You got him around here some-place?" she asked.

At the time, I had one large and expensive statue of Michael and archangel pins. She bought one of the pins and asked me if I had any information on Michael. Doreen Virtue's book *Archangels and Ascended Masters* was staring me in the eye from the bookshelves near the counter, so I grabbed it. Quickly thumbing through the table of contents, I found Michael on page thirty-three. I let her read about him while I waited on the other customers in the store. By the time I returned to Merrill, she was busy jotting down information about the archangel. As she continued to write, she told me that she had met with Michael in her dreams.

Merrill had lived alone in Scottsdale for many years in a condominium building. At the beginning, most of the others living there were single women like herself, but over the years a steady transition took place until she was the only original member there. Now the building was filled with young families that argued and fought. "The police are in my neighborhood almost as much as the mail carrier," she explained.

For several years, Merrill had thought about moving to Santa Fe, New Mexico, to be closer to a couple of her closest friends. "I'm not one to ask for advice," she said. "I usually take the bull by the horns and face the situation head on. Lately, though, I've been asking for help in knowing when to make the move. I mean, I don't ask anyone in particular, I just ask for help in my mind. That's why I'm here."

Merrill confided that she recently had three dreams where Michael appeared to her. "In the dreams, I am always sitting on a log near a beautiful stream with grass all around. The grass is so tall that it gently lies down around where I sit. Michael is radiant. He has deep blue eyes that match his blue tunic. His hair is as golden as freshly spun gold. His face is also gold, without any markings or blemishes. It's so beautiful. His eyes are soft yet piercing. He could look right through me if he wanted to. He could look through *all* of me, physically, spiritually and in every way!

"The last time he visited me, he again sat on the log next to me, but this time he spoke. He said, '*Merrill, when you want me, all you have to do is call my name.*' Oh, I tell you, when Michael looked at me as he spoke, he looked right through me! He made me feel so loved. Michael is such a beautiful man."

A few days later, Merrill reappeared at Angel Wings with a look of assurance in her eyes. She came in to buy *Archangels and Ascended Masters* and to tell me that she had made up her mind to move to Santa Fe as soon as she found a buyer for her condo. "Michael is with me," she told me. "I know that now and I am not ever alone."

CHAPTER ELEVEN

Angels on Fifth Avenue

When Pamela and I talked about our future, angels always came up in our conversation. Even before we moved to the Valley of the Sun, Pamela had started collecting angels and was intrigued with angel shops. On occasion, she would find a way to lure me to visit them with her, usually by inviting me to eat out afterwards. Over the years, we had felt the angels intervening in our lives, revealing their presence to us, caring for us and keeping us on track. With door number one and door number two now closed, we began to think about honoring the angels by opening an angel store. That way, we could bring the angels to the attention of as many people as possible. In the meantime, I called upon the angels to help me recognize that third door.

Near the beginning of our quest to find the right location for the art gallery we had planned to open, a business and financial advisor I had chosen said a little destination town would be the perfect fit for us, primarily because we didn't have a lot of funds available at the time. He thought the little historical town of Galena in the northwestern portion of Illinois near the Mississippi River would be the ideal spot for us. We weren't inclined to go there because Pamela and I wanted to be somewhere warm where we could see the sun shine on a more regular basis than it does in the upper Midwest.

Even so, we flew out to visit Galena a couple of times. Though just a city of thirty-five hundred folks, over eight hundred thousand people visit Galena every year. People come by the busloads from the Chicago area, the Twin Cities in Minnesota and the outlying areas. They come to Galena for three reasons: to shop, to eat and to shop. Then they get back on the bus and head for home.

Most of downtown Galena is made up of red brick buildings built before 1900. Galena's claim to fame is its connection to Ulysses S. Grant, who worked there in his father's leather store and also tried to be blacksmith. Some say he wasn't the best smithy. Others, however, felt he was pretty good at drinking bourbon. As you come into Galena's shopping district from the south, you see what I thought were two big green doors on either side of the street. As we walked the streets, we came upon a series of old photographs of men in rowboats paddling their way through town. The "doors," it turns out, were floodgates. My guess was that the town had been erected too close to Old Muddy.

That still didn't stop us from considering Galena, though. On our first visit, we found a great location right on Main Street. We connected with the property owners and discovered that not only was the store space available, but there was also a three-bedroom apartment right above it that we could rent. Imagine walking downstairs to go to work. Although we weren't quite ready to make the plunge, we had kept that place in the back of our minds. Now that I was free from my phone company job, we thought about Galena again. If our business and financial advisor had recommended it to us for an art gallery, why not an angel store?

We had considered opening a store in the Phoenix area, where we were now living, but the prospects weren't good. With three angel stores in the Phoenix valley, we didn't think another one would be viable. We pictured Scottsdale as an ideal place for our store, but a lady named Cathy already owned an angel store there, Angel Wings. We liked the name. It was one of those stores that Pamela would visit when she wanted to add to her angel collection. There was something about the store that kept calling us back. It was in a nice location, situated in a little courtyard just off the main shopping street.

While Phoenix didn't seem to have an opening for us, Galena, on the other hand, didn't yet have a store devoted exclusively to angels.

"How about Galena?" I finally said to Pamela.

Her face turned into a girlish pout. With her lower lip pushed up and out, she said, "I don't want to go back to the cold country." To be honest, I wasn't all that excited about going back either, but the business opportunity seemed good.

After a few more discussions, Pamela considered it a wise move too, and we would be only a few hours' drive from family and old friends.

"Let's call the landlord of that great store location we checked on last year and see what's available now," she said.

"You're on," I replied. I dug out her telephone number and gave the woman a call. The apartment was still available, but the store had been rented out. She told us of some store vacancies on the street and said we should hurry and check them out before they were taken. That night, Pamela booked us a flight to Chicago so we could do our research in Galena. We were set to leave on March 2.

The day before our departure, Pamela was at her job as an administrative assistant to the principal of Finley Farms Elementary School in Gilbert and I was doing some last-minute shopping before we flew to Illinois. I found myself near Fifth Avenue in downtown Scottsdale near the angel store. I decided to stop in because I wanted to ask Cathy about the vendors she did business with and Pamela wanted me to see if she had a mahogany angel to replace the one that had flown off the top of our TV and broken her wing.

As I walked in the front door, Cathy was just coming out of her little reading room.

"Hi, my name is Jerry. I've been in your store before and I was wondering if you could help me out."

She had a bewildered look on her face as she studied mine.

"I'm going to Galena, Illinois—"

"Galena?" she interrupted. "I just finished a reading with a gal from Galena."

"Well, I came in to ask you for the names of the vendors you do business with for your shop, because we are opening an angel store in Galena. I also want to buy an angel for my wife."

"Why Galena?"

"Because you have the only angel store here we would be interested in."

Cathy folded her hands together in front of her and calmly

said, "Well, did you know that my store is for sale?"

My mind went blank, my eyes glazed over and I could feel my jaw falling somewhere around my rib cage.

I stumbled out of the store and around the corner to where the car was parked. I sat down on the passenger's side and called Pam, still in shock.

"Honey," I said, "you won't believe what just happened."

We canceled our flight and exactly one month later, on April 1, 2002, Angel Wings was ours. I had quit the phone company on February 1, found an angel store for sale on March 1, and was a store owner by April 1. Both of us were ecstatic. We didn't have to go back to the cold country and we could stay in our own house here. Door number three had opened and we walked through it with faith. The angel reading I had done in the tiny hotel room in Utah couldn't have been more accurate.

Cathy asked if she could stay on and do angel readings with her clients until she found a place of her own to continue her readings. "Of course," I said, and she did stay for a short time. I learned that Cathy was certified to do angel readings under the tutelage of Dr. Doreen Virtue. I asked Cathy if she used the oracle cards and she answered quickly, "Only if the client wants me to use the cards, or if the angels tell me to use them." Hmm, I thought, the angels talk to her. Interesting. People come to her for insight just as they go to palm readers and the like, except Cathy has an in with the angels. Until our conversation that day, I didn't know of another soul who did angel readings in that way.

Just two months after moving into the store, another opportunity opened. A Mexican furniture store nearby was moving to a mall. Their space, on Fifth Avenue, was owned by the same landlord we had and he had no problem at all with Angel Wings moving into the vacated spot on the avenue. In fact, he had wanted the store there for quite some time, but Cathy had been content to leave it right where it was.

It was scary for us to consider that move. Our rent would more than double, and with our limited finances, that was huge. But, true to the angelic guidance I had received in the reading, we took the leap of faith. By letting go and trusting the "angel nudges," we were in our new location by July. Over the course of those two months, we had to invest much more in remodeling the interior of the building than I had anticipated, but in the end, it was worth it. Angel Wings looked bigger, brighter and happier than ever. The positive feedback from our customers was and still is gratifying. We wanted to create a place where people could enjoy a sense of peace, love, hope and serenity and be able to take that special feeling with them as they left Angel Wings.

There's one more important part of the story. Our store has two doors. The front door is located on Fifth Avenue. The other is right on the courtyard. We finally understood the prophetic message behind meeting the lady in lavenders in Lahaina who spoke of believing in angels as we sat with her in a little courtyard just off the main street.

One morning shortly after opening the store, a young woman came in carrying a bundle of colorful flyers. She was tall with long legs and a short skirt. Her flowing red hair matched her blouse, made of a bright orange lacy material with hues of light blues and a hint of red. She strolled over to the counter and handed me a flyer.

"My name is Gina, and I take it you are the new owner," she said.

"Yes, I'm Jerry. And what is it that you do?"

"Angel readings," she said softly yet excitedly. "I am putting on a seminar on how to connect with your angels. It will include meditations and teach people how to meditate and make contact with Spirit, and we will practice angel readings."

"How are you going to practice angel readings?" I asked.

"After I guide the group through meditation, I will talk about how I do readings. Then I'll pair up everyone and they will practice with each other," she said.

"Cool, Gina!" I said. "Where did you learn how to do readings?"

"Oh, I went to Doreen Virtue's Angel Therapy Practitioner's Course in Laguna Beach," she said confidently.

"That's amazing. You've got guts."

It sounded good to me, and I liked her appearance and personality.

"I'll hand out the flyers to my customers," I said. I took a bundle of her flyers and put them in an information rack in front of the store. "Come back and tell me how it turned out, won't you?"

"Oh, I'll be back," she said matter-of-factly. She smiled, turned toward the door and waved goodbye.

By the time Gina returned, Pamela and I had made our move to Fifth Avenue, just twenty-nine feet west. Gina opened the courtyard door, walked in about half way and twirled around.

"Whoa, I really like what you've done here. I didn't realize you were moving," she said.

"We didn't either, but the opportunity presented itself and we couldn't turn it down. There's still some work to be done, but we'll make it a comfortable home for our angels," I said, still in the process of getting the store in order. "How was the seminar?

"Oh, I was hoping there would have been more people in attendance," she said with a sigh.

"So where do you do your angel readings?" I asked.

"Right now I do them two days a week at a little boutique in North Scottsdale and I'm looking for another place as well." Gina's energy felt as if it came right from her heart.

"Would you like to do angel readings here, Gina?"

"I'd love to!" she said.

"Great. I'll need help making a special room in the store for the readings and also a place where folks can just sit and read books, monthlies and magazines."

"No problem," Gina said. "I would be very happy to do that for you—and I would like to bless this store and everything in it."

"It's a done deal, lady!" I said, surprising myself a little. A few years earlier, I would have cringed at the thought of "blessing" something or someone. Too strong of a religious tone for me. Gina's offer, however, felt sweet in a pure way, a spiritual way. She was willing to do it from her heart and her heart alone, and that was a refreshing thought—someone blessing our little angel store who happened not to be a man wearing all black with a little white collar and a look of "you owe me" in his eyes.

I brought in a big white fountain with two large cherubs sitting atop it (a gift from our three children) and placed it near an inner wall a few feet from the store's entrance. Gina had a great idea of putting some stones on a table next to the fountain so people could choose one and place it in the fountain. She designed a sign that read: *Cast an Angel Blessing: Please take a stone and offer your angel blessing into the fountain.*

Even before owning the angel store, a vision came to me one day while I was meditating to have a prayer bowl somewhere within the store I would someday own. The prayer bowl would be there for those who needed prayers themselves or who wanted prayers said for their friends or loved ones. So we also set up a prayer bowl in Angel Wings. Almost daily, someone will add a special, heartfelt prayer to that bowl. The sign next to the bowl reads: *All the prayers asked for here are prayed for within twenty-four hours.* Every day, either Pamela or I pray for the intentions that have been placed in that bowl. We also pray for those who have taken the time to add their prayer intentions to the bowl, asking that they be blessed with health, wealth and happiness.

With our new angel fountain and prayer bowl in place, Gina, Pamela and I had a special evening where we walked every inch of the store as Gina "smudged" (burned special herbs to clear lower energies, a tradition derived from a Native American sacred ritual) and blessed all aspects of our new little corner of Eden on Fifth Avenue.

We celebrated the event by sipping champagne and listening to angel music. We talked about the store's positive effect on people, taking in what we had created, and we thanked the angels for their guidance and love. They had led us to this place and we knew they had something special in store for this store and for us.

Gina stayed with us for several months, giving her angel readings and helping the store evolve. During the slow time of the hot desert summer days, I would see her sitting cross-legged at the reading table, softly caressing, shuffling and laying out the angel oracle cards created by Doreen Virtue. Occasionally, I would have her do a reading for me. She would graciously oblige.

"Do you mind if I give it a try?" I asked one day.

"Not at all. You will be giving readings soon too," she said nonchalantly.

"I will, huh?" I said, recalling the mini-reading I had done on the retiring pilot in Utah.

She encouraged me to continue doing readings, and I did. I called those readings practice and just let the energy flow. I shuffled the cards until they clumped together, then laid the deck face down and pulled out the number of cards I felt the angels were prompting me to choose. I placed them face down on the table, one at a time. Then I would turn them up, one at a time, and intuit the meaning of each card for her.

Gina was only at the store three days a week and I wanted an angel reader there every day. While I was looking for other angel readers who had participated in Doreen Virtue's Angel Therapy Practitioner course, I pulled out a resumé left by a gentleman named Robert. He had light blondish-brown hair, stood around five foot ten and was thin and in his thirties. He reminded me a lot of Niles, the brother of TV's Frazier. Robert had studied with teachers I was not familiar with, so I asked him to give me a reading over the phone first before considering him. What convinced me most about his abilities as a reader was the answer I received from him concerning my daughter, Alicia.

"Do you have any information about my daughter?" I asked.

"She's healing right now. She needs more time for her stomach area to heal—"

I hadn't said anything to him at the time about Alicia's health, but she was indeed recovering from emergency surgery on a ruptured ovary she had had two weeks earlier. I interrupted him mid-sentence and said, "You're hired."

One day while things were quiet at the store, Robert was sitting at the table in the reading room and I was at the counter doing some reordering. Suddenly I got a gut feeling, an intuitive hit, a message, whatever you want to call it, that I should give Robert a reading. I put aside the catalog I was working with and walked over to the reading room.

"Robert, do you mind if I give you a reading?" His eyes shot up at me with a bewildered look. Half laughing, he put his arms up in the air, as if surrendering, and said, "Sure, why not?"

So I sat down across from him at the table, grabbed the deck of forty-four angel cards and started to shuffle. As I did so, I received another intuitive hit: rather than use the cards, just put them down in front of you and start talking about what you feel.

I rattled on for about twenty minutes. Robert sat in silence. After the automatic words stopped coming, I stopped. The reading had ended. I was flabbergasted. Where had those words or ideas come from? Card readings, yes, but never had I done a reading just with my gut—or was it "just with my gut"? As soon as that thought crossed my mind, Robert spoke.

"That was really good, Jerrrrry," he said somewhat inquisitively. "I didn't know you could read."

"Me neither."

I didn't know what else to say. Besides, I had a customer to wait on.

Later that day, Robert left the store and peddled his bike to the bus stop on Camelback Road to continue his journey home. Once he reached home, he called me back at the store. He said he couldn't shake the messages from the reading. They had touched him deeply, and he wanted to reiterate his thanks. He said the messages had helped him refocus on the positive and let go of the negativity in his life.

Great, I thought, but those messages weren't my words; they had come directly from the Spirit world. I may have been the conduit but, truthfully, I didn't even remember what I had said a few hours earlier. That's still the way it is with me. After a little while, I don't recall the readings.

One summer's day, while Pamela was also at the store going over the books, realigning some of the angel figurines we sell and neatening up after me (the store needs a woman's touch), who should walk into Angel Wings but Judy Peters, the bereavement coordinator from Hospice of Arizona, with her husband, John. Judy is also a hypnotherapist.

There were hugs all around. We chatted, mostly catching up with each other, and then angel readings came into the conversation. Judy loved angels too. In fact, I always thought she was an angel in disguise.

"Doreen Virtue is presenting an Angel Therapy Practitioner course in Laguna Beach in October," Pamela mentioned. "Judy, why don't you go?"

"I'll go if Jerry goes," Judy replied.

"Okay," I shot back. I couldn't believe what I had just heard myself say. What had I gotten myself into now?

The course turned out to be a fantastic experience. There were 115 of us in attendance and I was one of only eight men.

Each day started with a yoga session, and vegan food was provided for us every day. All of us were eager to learn how to do angel readings by receiving messages from the angels. Dr. Doreen Virtue was an inspired teacher. We practiced giving each other readings, changing partners each time. For my third practice session, my partner was a petite black-haired earth angel from Venezuela. English was her second language and she read me first. She immediately saw a small dog in my living space.

"I'm sorry," I said. "We don't have a dog at our house. We have old Stanley, though; he's a sixteen-year-old flea-bitten farm cat."

She had a determined look on her face as she kept talking.

"Yes, you have a dog in your life, a small dog with curly hair and her name is…." She stuttered a bit, trying to come up with the name. "Pique, or Piqway? Something like that, anyway," she said.

"Well, I don't have a dog—wait a sec. Yes, I do! My daughter just got a puppy and her name is Pixie," I blurted out. Amazing, I thought, simply amazing. Here is this woman from a foreign country who speaks a foreign language, sitting with someone she has never seen before, and she could see and give me the name of the dog that had just entered my life a few days before I had come to Laguna Beach! I had doubted her, but all along she knew she was right. She knew that angels don't lie. I know that now too. The angels never lie. We may forget or choose not to remember, but the angels know. The angels always know.

Early on during the course, we were given an assignment. We were to think of all the things in our lives that we were tired of or wanted to get rid of, things that kept us from moving toward Spirit or our higher selves—such as old habits or negative thought patterns—and write them down on a piece of paper. The class was then instructed to go down to the beach and to pick up something like a small stick, rock or seashell. We were to take the paper on which we had written our intentions, wrap it around the object and place it near us. Some placed it on their night stand, others carried it in their pockets or set it next to them throughout the days. I put mine under my pillow.

The last evening of the course, we participated in a releasing ceremony on the beach as we collectively burned the papers in a bonfire. Then, with ceremonial drumbeating, we marched single file to the water's edge and threw into the ocean the object that symbolically held the old patterns that were no longer serving us. It was a sign that we would forevermore be free from old thought processes that had kept us from moving in a more spiritual direction, away from the ego (the lower self).

That course gave me the confidence to continue along the path I had been shown, the path the angels wanted me to walk. Who would have thought that I'd be giving angel readings and that all sorts of people would be coming to me for those readings—young and old and in between, male and female, doctors, counselors, nuns, professionals, anyone seeking advice or seeking messages from their own angels or even from their loved ones who had passed over. Who would have guessed that I would soon be helping other people free themselves from fear, open up to their Source, by whatever name they call it, and move closer to the angels?

A Fall into Knowing

Jillian came into the store to look for an angel pin to wear on her lapel. As she made her purchase, she asked me if I believed in angels. I nodded yes and told her that many of my customers do too, and sometimes they even tell me stories of their encounters with angels. She went on to tell me hers.

Jillian had a near-death experience when she fell from her horse in New Mexico on a rocky trail. She immediately went toward the light. She was given information, through what she called "enlightened communication," about how to live, her purpose here and how we are to love one another. Jillian also received information on reincarnation and learned that the angelic realm is truly a part of God. She told me, with a trace of sadness in her voice, that since her accident, her family and friends had distanced themselves from her, as if she didn't fit in with them any longer.

"Actually," I told her, looking into her eyes, "just the opposite has occurred. *They* no longer fit in with *you*. You have moved beyond them and their views and comprehensions. They no longer know how to relate to you. In reality, they are distancing themselves from the unknown.

"Don't be frightened. Trust yourself and the dance movements within your heart. Do not doubt, but rather let go of fear. In the end, you must continually seek peace. Through that door, you will find the goal: *love*."

Jillian's eyes brightened. She lifted her head, looked me in the eye and said, "That's what I think too. I never thought I'd hear my own thoughts spoken back to me. I will nurture myself and give thanks for my time to love on this brilliant star." She thanked me and gave me a big, warm hug. Then she turned and, with pride and confidence in her walk, strolled out of Angel Wings.

CHAPTER TWELVE

Angel Readings

When you watch TV or movies or read the newspaper, so much of it is about ego, our lower selves, and the fear factor. On the other hand, in the angelic realm and the Spirit world, everything is vibrating and humming at a higher frequency, and everyone there is tuned in to their higher self, free from ego. While we seem to be obsessed with fear, even fear about the spiritual world, God and the angels have only unconditional love for us. Love cannot be tainted, diluted, altered or cut in half. Therefore, there can be no fear when love is all there is. Since that is true, why should we fear God, angels or Spirit?

I get a kick out of the fear factor I sometimes see in the people who step into Angel Wings. Since we moved the store up on the avenue, in the heart of downtown Scottsdale, many vacationers, tourists, locals and retired folks shuffle up and down the streets. Many wander in, not knowing what to expect. Most people love the store and tell us so straight out. Those who don't care for angels—or, better stated, those who are afraid of angels—scoot out the door faster than they came in.

One day, for example, an elderly couple stepped in, the silver-haired wife in the lead and her husband lagging behind. She stopped and, through her glasses, peered up and down the aisles, to the walls and back around to the front. Then she did an about face and said to her husband, "It's all angels, Harold! Let's get out of here!" And just like that, they were gone. Franklin Delano Roosevelt said it best back at his inauguration in 1933: "The only thing we have to fear is fear itself."

Others who come to Angel Wings are mesmerized by the relaxing, meditative music and ambience of the shop. They hang out just to browse in a safe haven away from all the nonsense outside "in the real world," as they say. Some walk through the doors just so they can step into the air conditioning for a moment and then they realize where they are, or maybe they want to get change for a dollar to slip into the drink machines dotted all around Old Town. Whatever it is that draws visitors to our doors and our hearts, I am at peace and happy.

Of course, I too had to deal with the fear factor, especially when I started doing angel readings on my own. The ego doesn't like it when its grip is loosened and we become more in tune with our higher self, the God-self that resides within. There were times in the beginning when I was worried that I would sit down to do a reading and nothing would happen. I doubted myself. My mind would kick into high gear and I would find myself thinking, "Am I making all this up?" But each reading does come from my higher self, and the angels are always there to give me encouragement and strength and to expand their wings of knowledge and love to bring their messages to my clients. They are so loving, so kind. As I explain to my clients, angels are the arms and hands of God. They do God's work here on earth.

After I worked through the fear factor, the readings became second nature to me, and I always prepare myself with a ritual that helps me make the connection. I prefer to meditate for at least half an hour before people arrive for their scheduled readings. If I have scheduled two, three or more readings in a row, before each reading I call in Michael archangel to clear my chakras. I begin every reading by asking Michael to be present and to remove all negativity and ego-based thought. I also invite the Holy Spirit to be with us to ensure the clarity of the messages being transferred from the client's angels to my angels to me.

When I began providing clients with angel sessions, I would enter the little café directly behind the store in the Kiva Center Courtyard, and the hostess would do a double take as I walked in. She would tell me that at first glance she had seen a taller male with me. Then, in a blink of an eye, he'd be gone. This happened more than once and with different hosts. I'd like to think it was Michael who was by my side.

Michael has been absolutely magnificent to me. He has never let me down. He allows me to relax and be confident and clear to transmit the messages that the angels want each person to hear. His presence also puts the clients at ease, which creates a nurturing environment, giving way to a higher receptivity.

Angel therapy sessions are as varied as the clients who come to receive them. Many times, I will receive messages from angels, guides, ascended masters or loved ones who have passed on. These messengers all look to me like the negatives of photos. When the ascended masters—such as Mother Mary, Kuan Yin,

Buddha, Krishna, Mary Magdalene and Jesus—present themselves, a deep, profound, silent love fills the room. Along with
seeing their negative-like outlines, I also feel the presence of
these spiritual beings and see what I describe as their energy
forms. The forms of energy are round, about the size of a basketball, but not rigid. They are always rotating and look like a
radiant ball of many colors.

When I am doing an angel reading, at times I also see symbols. I don't know what these symbols represent, but they always
mean something to the client. I tell my clients in advance that
this sometimes happens so they can be aware of it. During one
session, for example, I saw a silver streak and when I told my
client about it, she said, "Oh, that's my grandpa. He had white
hair and moved quickly, so he was nicknamed the Silver Streak."
In another session, a spoon appeared before me in front of my
third-eye chakra, and the young lady who was my client said,
"That would be my grandmother. I loved her dearly and she
practically raised me as a child. I feel her presence often."

As I said earlier, I seldom remember what takes place during
the readings, although a certain few are permanently etched in
my memory. I do, for example, remember the first reading I ever
gave as a Certified Angel Therapist, the term for someone who
has finished Dr. Doreen Virtue's Angel Therapy Practitioner's
course. The reading was for a man in his early fifties. The gentleman came in with his girlfriend and wanted her to be present
for the reading too. I didn't mind, but at the same time I
informed him that I pass on the information I receive regardless
of what it is the angels have to offer. The messages, I said, would
be specifically for him, for his healing and guidance. He still
wanted his girlfriend there. The man asked no specific ques-

tions; all he wanted from me was to see what I could tell him about himself. Fair enough—a test, I thought, and proceeded.

As the session began, I asked him to take a few deep breaths with me. I said, "Inhale the spirit of the angels and exhale out all toxins." After calling on Michael archangel and the Holy Spirit for the clarity of the messages from his angels to mine, the reading began. I intuited what his angels wanted conveyed to him— that he was a healer and that when he was a younger man, he had been in Vietnam in a Marine outfit. The man shook his head negatively. How odd, I thought. The angels always tell the truth, yet he was denying that this was true.

The angels continued and became quite chatty. They told me he was a voyeur, a person who liked to watch. That took me back a bit and I almost started laughing. I didn't know quite how to take it or interpret it, especially with his girlfriend sitting by his side. That reading was an eye opener for me. His girlfriend was sitting right there and yet the angels didn't hold back anything. When I told the man that he was at a crossroads in his life and that he was "an observer of people," a student of people and situations (which is how I put it), he got fidgety. We reached the half hour that he had requested and we agreed to end the session.

Immediately following the session, the man told me that he had been a chiropractor but had left that field. He now had enough money so that he didn't ever have to work again and was happy just traveling, but he was feeling compelled to help others in some way. He went on to explain that he had, in fact, been in Vietnam, as the angels told me, but as a navy medic attached to a marine unit. Even though he was at one time a medic and then a chiropractor, he had never seen himself as a healer. All I

could think of at that moment were three things: people sometimes simply forget, they are in denial and angels never lie.

Since I began giving readings just a few years ago, Mary,
mother of Jesus, has appeared several times during the readings.
It doesn't matter if the client is alone with me or if his or her
friends are in the room. Mary will appear, usually facing their
right side in a kneeling and praying position. When Mary is
present, a special feeling pervades the room. I become very
aware of my breathing and feel as though I'm partially out of my
body and surrounded by God's pure love and light. It's such a
profound and loving experience that the hair on my arms stands
up and I get gooseflesh. The readings with Mary are also different from other readings in that my client usually notices an
aroma in the reading room. The client will often tell me of the
distinct smell of roses in the room.

Part of the message Mary always conveys to the clients is
that she knows and understands their hurt, their anguish and
the feelings they have stuffed inside in an effort to forget what
has happened to them. In every case where Mary has come, with
only one exception, the client has lost a child through an accident, illness or an abortion. How the child died matters not to
Mary; she is there because she, too, lost her child. I tell the
clients that they are not alone and that God loves them uncon-
ditionally, regardless of what happened. That is the message that
Mary carries to them.

In the reading where Mary came to someone who hadn't lost
a child, I was at first confused when I felt Mary enter the room
because I didn't sense that the client had children. The woman
before me was in her late fifties with dark hair, a roundish figure

and no makeup. She wore a dark pair of slacks, a gray-colored blouse and a long necklace with a pendant around her neck. I told the woman that I felt the presence of Mother Mary on her right side. My client nodded. As I continued the reading, the message I received from Spirit was that this woman had worked with children, was deeply devoted to caring for others and was connected to a religious sect. After the reading, the woman told me she had been a nun for many years and loved what she did.

Sometimes the angel readings turn out to be whimsical. As the old adage goes, angels can fly because they take themselves lightly. These kinds of angel readings are intended to help the client lighten up, to take life as it comes and to not be so serious. Sometimes fairies appear to remind clients to take a deep breath, explore nature more and revere the environment. The fairies live in nature among the trees, shrubs, bushes, grass, streams and rivers. They come to show the client that they can learn and do more by being outside of man-made buildings and by being in touch with the elements. They send the message that we are all connected; people, animals, rocks, mountains, water—everything is made of molecules. An ancient Hawaiian saying expresses this sentiment: "Go easy, brudda. Like the trees, hills and all the fish in the sea, you're supposed to be here too."

Some readings can be difficult when people put up blocks or shields that simply cannot be penetrated, usually out of fear. They are afraid of what might be shown to them, such as a perceived shortcoming or a bad experience they had as a child. A part of them doesn't want to rehash a bad scene in their life or to know that there are lessons to be learned from the past.

One reading in particular was difficult right from the beginning. I almost ended the session before it began, but a voice inside of me said to keep going. The man had positioned himself so he was sitting almost sideways and was looking at me out of the corner of his eyes. It was as if he was trying to look away yet keep an eye on me at the same time. Leonard was large and stocky. His hair, short, thick and more gray than brown, was in disarray and it lay down in several directions. He wore blue jeans and an old, worn T-shirt. Leonard had questions right from the beginning, but he had trouble putting them into words. Halfway into a question, his central point would change, making it difficult for me to follow along. I asked that before I entertained any questions, we both take several deep breaths together and exhale slowly.

I closed my eyes and took three deep cleansing breaths and let them out slowly. He remained silent, and then shot another question my way: "How does this work?" I began by telling Leonard about Michael archangel and the Holy Spirit and how my angels relay messages to me from his angels.

"No, no, *no!*" he moaned loudly. "I don't believe in angels or God." Then why the heck did you come to me for a reading, I thought to myself. After all, you came here for an angel reading, and the angels are always my connection to get these spiritual readings. Instead, I said nothing; I didn't want to rile this oversized gnome. At first, I didn't know what to do. My mind, already spinning, suddenly quieted and became crystal clear. I sensed a voice within me say, "Ask him if the terms *higher self* and *Spirit* are okay to use in place of *God* and *angels*." When I did, he hesitantly nodded a silent yes. The way he was squinting and peering at me sideways, I didn't know whether he would settle in for the reading or just reach over and grab me by the throat. We began.

As the reading progressed, he watched me closely, his head still slightly turned to one side or the other, almost never looking at me face-to-face. When something came up that he didn't want to hear, he would boom, "No, no, *no!*" again. Of course, there always happened to be several customers close by when he did. Something tells me they may never come back. The reading was an hour long, although it seemed much longer, as I had to be constantly aware of how I worded the messages from his angels.

The session ended quietly. We walked out of the reading room and over to the counter. I thanked him for coming in and gave him a big hug, reminding him that he is always loved and never alone. At this point, Leonard seemed mellow. He accepted the words and thanked me, then ambled out of Angel Wings.

A couple of weeks passed by. Then one day, as I was sitting on a small folding chair near the back entrance, I saw a long shadow on the floor moving toward me from the front of the store. I looked up. At first glance, I thought I was watching a linebacker for the Green Bay Packers barreling down the aisle toward me with a football in his hands. My heart started pounding. Suddenly I realized it was Leonard carrying a watermelon.

He smiled with the biggest toothed grin I'd ever seen, gaps in his teeth and all. All aglow and looking as happy as a child with a lollypop, he said, "I can't tell you how much you helped. I've never felt better in my entire life. You were so nice to welcome me into your store. Not only that, but you made me feel like a complete and whole human being. I am happy to be me now and I want to thank you by giving you this watermelon. It's completely organic." Leonard was wearing a clean T-shirt and new blue jeans and it looked as if he had just come from the barbershop. There wasn't a hair out of place. He reached out with those long arms that had been cradling the watermelon and handed me his gift. I accepted it and set it on the counter.

"You know, you're full of God's love right now," I told him. Leonard gave me such a big hug that I thought my ribs would cave in. He thanked me again and started for the front door.

"It wasn't me, you know," I shouted after him. "The love for you is in the universe and I'm just the conduit in between. I had nothing to do with it."

He stopped in his tracks and slowly turned back, pointing a finger at me. "Oh no," he said. "You had everything to do with it. I'll never forget what you've done for me. My life has meaning now." In an instant, he was gone. I never saw the guy again. I felt a little like a country doctor just then—in lieu of money for services, I'd been paid with fruit.

A year after we opened the store, Gina said good-bye to Angel Wings and lit out across the desert for greener pastures in sunny California. She had done such a fantastic job at the store with her blessing, her angel readings and her natural red-haired presence and beauty. Robert, knowing that I intended to do angel readings myself as well as run the store, now felt free to move on to Tucson to be closer to his mother. We had something in common, old Robert and me—a love and longing for Hawaii. He stopped in the store before leaving for Tucson and handed me a note. On it he had scribbled the name of a book. I tried to read it.

"*The Secretion and My Stories—*"

"No, no, no," he said. "It's *The Secrets and Mysteries of Hawaii.*"

"Oh, I'm sorry. I can't read your writing worth a darn."

"I can't think of the author right now, but look it up on the Internet. You'll find it there. You might like the book. I know how much you want to get back there."

"Well, Robert, I know you do too. I'll tell you what. Between you and me, whoever gets there first wins."

Wins what?"

"You don't win *anything*. You just win!"

Robert chuckled and shook his head. He thanked Pamela and me for having him at the store, saying we had made him feel like family. I believe Robert did feel comfortable with us, more comfortable than he had felt for quite some time. Mahalo, Robert. Aloha.

I followed Robert's advice, found the book and the author's website on the Internet and purchased *The Secrets and Mysteries of Hawaii*. Funny things began to happen at the store as I read about the mysteries of Hawaii. I have a five-disc CD changer programmed for random selections. I fill it with music that is meditative and spiritual. Hawaiian music is the most spiritual music for me and one of the discs contained beautiful Hawaiian melodies. In between customers, whenever I would continue to read *The Secrets and Mysteries of Hawaii* by Pila of Hawaii, the Hawaiian music would come on. Then something even more unusual happened.

While reading a section about a particular place on the Big Island near the Parker cattle ranch, three ladies came in the courtyard door at the back of the store. As they did, one of them commented on the Hawaiian music. She sat down on the stool in front of the counter and asked about it. I explained that the music always came on while I was reading this book by Pila, and

I mentioned that I was now reading about the area near the cattle ranch. She had a startled look on her face. "That's where I grew up!" she said. She went on to tell me that her father had worked on the cattle ranch and that she was born and spent her life right at the location described in the book.

During this time when I was immersing myself in Pila's book, someone would walk into the store wearing a Hawaiian shirt and the CD changer would start playing the Hawaiian music again. I would always ask the people if they had ever visited Hawaii. It never failed that they would either have a story about the Islands or had lived there.

Pila and I have since become email friends. He is part shaman, part Cherokee, a lecturer and a master of Hawaiian history. I hold close his words of guidance. Mahalo, big guy. Oorah. As it turned out, Pila of Hawaii and Dannion Brinkley, the author who wrote about his near-death experiences, are both ex-marines and had served tours in Vietnam. I, too, had served in Vietnam, in an army infantry unit within the 25th Infantry Division, which is headquartered at Schofield Barracks on the island of Oahu. I have yet to visit it. *Oorah* is a term used by the marines as a reminder of fellowship, of their brotherhood, if you will.

That longing, loving feeling for Hawaii is still strong in my heart, and it has been calling me back to the Islands for quite some time. Not long after I finished reading Pila's book, the angels led me to a series of new experiences and adventures that would at last reveal why.

Replacing Evil with Love

Meredith was visiting in the area with a friend and said she was guided to come into Angel Wings but didn't know why. She thought maybe I could help her figure out the reason she had been drawn here. I told Meredith that many people come through our doors. Some have heard of the store, others are buying a gift for a friend who believes in angels and others are just curious. Now and then, I explained, a person comes by because they have been touched by angels.

Meredith focused her eyes on her hands as she held her keys and purse. She softly raised her eyes to mine and said, "I was never touched by an angel, but I have a fairy story." I encouraged her to share it with me.

"I don't know why I'm telling you this," she said, but continued on anyway. "I was raised in a very abusive family. My brother, sister and I were abused physically, emotionally and sexually on the family farm in Iowa. Even my mother was extremely abusive, and we all wound up in therapy. My brother and I became nurses, while my sister left the farm and came out here to Mesa over thirty years ago. She left as soon as the law would let her leave.

"My brother and I cared for our father as he went through cancer several years ago. Both of us were able to come to terms with the past and to forgive him completely. My father was at peace too. It was a healing experience for my brother and me. Our sister couldn't make it back to see my father as he was dying. She didn't come back for our mother's death or her funeral either. That's what I want to tell you about, my mother's death.

"Ten years ago, she was in the early stages of Alzheimer's disease. My brother and I also cared for her near the end. We were fortunate enough to have the help we needed so that she never had to leave the Iowa farmhouse where we were raised. On the last day of her life, as my mother lay on her deathbed, I gazed out the bedroom window and I saw them."

"Saw what?" I gently asked.

"I saw fairies. Fairies appeared everywhere on the farm where the sexual, physical or emotional abuse had taken place. As I looked out at the old tractor shed, I saw a fairy hovering near one corner. The same thing happened when I looked at the milk house, the barn and parts of the yard and pastures. Inside the house, too, wherever evil had lurked, the fairies appeared. I had the sense that all the evil was being removed and replaced with a light of love. I don't know how else to explain it to you. As the fairies appeared at each site, the awful evil was gone."

Continuing on in her straightforward way, Meredith said, "Something else happened. We had never had deer on the property at the near end of the field that was directly in front of the bedroom area of our house. But as my mother breathed her last, right at that very spot in the field, another place where my brother and I had both been abused, not just one deer appeared but several. They stood there and looked up at the window as my brother and I looked back at them. None of us had ever seen deer there before. Then my mother breathed her last breath and she was gone."

CHAPTER THIRTEEN

Taking a Deep Breath

Being from the upper Midwest, you're more likely to learn how to break down and clean a hunting rifle than trust something new because, well, you just never know. But the angels were at it again, intent on breaking down my old barriers, pushing me to try new things. Their next nudge came by way of something I was a little shy about and unsure of—past-life regressions. As I read about past-life regressions, they piqued my interest. I was ready for more, but I was timid at first.

Pamela and I decided to venture into this unknown territory together. We got our first taste of a regression at a bookstore in Mesa, Arizona, where we attended a workshop on hypnosis and past-life regressions by a well-known psychologist who was an expert in hypnotherapy. We sat as far back in the audience as we could and near an exit in case the psychologist decided to pick someone from the audience to stand up front and wanted to do something weird to them under hypnosis. You know how it is.

A bookstore seemed an odd place to experience past-life

regressions, I thought, but I guess if you have written a book on the subject, you could get much better results by demonstrating rather than telling about what you do. Even from the back row, it seemed to be the right time for a new experience and possibly even a life-changing, mind-altering journey into the unknown. It was time to dig deeper into the truth.

Ready or not, our group of over fifty eager novices closed our eyes and cleared our conscious minds. The hypnotherapist then led us down three flights of stairs, each step bringing us closer to a door. When we reached the door, the door to the unknown, we were to open it. What happened from that point on was up to each of us. He gave us only one instruction—to look down at ourselves to see what we were wearing and to notice if there was a calendar we could see.

I walked through an old, moss-covered wooden door with guarded excitement. As I looked down, I felt myself looking through the eyes of a child. I saw myself dressed in clothing made of brown heavy burlap. It was stitched on the sides and hung down from my neck in a dress-like fashion. I was a young boy, maybe twelve years of age, and I was barefooted. I was standing there alone, looking down, with no feelings at all—no feelings of love or of being loved. No anger either. That's as far as I got in my first past-life regression. I had gone back to a time when I was young and alone, but it wasn't clear what time it was. I felt nothing more.

Pamela, however, went a little deeper and a little farther. The thought of what she might experience in a past-life regression frightened her, but that day she was feeling comfortable in her surroundings and ready for whatever would come her way.

"I was still a little hesitant as I walked down that long flight of stairs," she told me, "but once that door opened, I stepped forward and saw a whole different world. I was in my late twenties. As I looked down, I saw that I was barefoot, dressed in a burlap dress, my hair a tad disheveled. The next thing I saw and heard was so vivid and disturbing that it brought me to tears.

"I was in a small town that had narrow dirt streets and run-down wood homes, huts and other small buildings. I was standing on our front porch with my small son, who was maybe around seven years old, when a wagon pulled by horses came flying around the corner on two wheels, looking as if it was going to roll over. I sensed terror. A soldier grabbed my arm and threw me into the rear of the wagon, where at least six others, mostly women, were crouching. I immediately hung on to the nearest arm. We huddled together with a feeling of immense terror, trying to gain strength by clinging to one another. My son ran after me, screaming and crying, both of us reaching for the other, but to no avail.

"Then I saw myself being put on a platform, tied to a pole with my hands behind me and burned at the stake. The smoke and flames engulfed me in seconds. Spectators were watching the event with cheers and merriment, as if it was the best form of entertainment they could imagine. I understood that I was one of many who had been vocal in speaking the truth, a truth the local authorities wanted to eliminate.

"When the hypnotherapist guided us back up the stairs and into the now, I found myself back in the bookstore with the rest of the people seated in the audience. I could still feel the warmth of tears running down my cheeks. I didn't feel fear, but I did feel a little sadness, as if I had read a very sad story."

The author continued his talk on past-life regression and its purpose. Before the workshop, neither Pam nor I knew that past-life regressions (or PLRs, as they are called) were being used as a healing technique. Not only can the regressions be a tool for growth and spiritual exploration, but they can also help people with problems such as addictions, phobias and limited beliefs. They can help to remove negative patterns and ease the pain that has been placed upon us from other people, places and situations from the past. Hypnosis is used in past-life regressions to dig deep into the subconscious and get to the root of a problem and its solution.

After the past-life regression at the bookstore, I found myself attending other group sessions as they became available. Those group regressions gave me a deeper understanding of myself as well as a certain self-assuredness that I felt had been lacking prior to the PLRs. They also gave me a new and positive way of looking at our culture's and the world's mores from the standpoint of reincarnation. The refusal to believe in reincarnation in much of the Western world's culture and religions began to make me chuckle.

Profound eye openers, the regressions gave me a broader sense of reasoning, a clearer knowing of God, the works of God, and the way the past, present and future collide to create the now. At this point in my life, I felt as if I was really learning, flying through the sky, noticing the glittering sparkles of angel dust and picking up speed as I bathed in the beauty of the universe. Clutching the handles of the rollercoaster car of past-life regressions, I braced for more new insights coming my way.

As I went to group regressions with psychotherapists and certified hypnotherapists, one thing did not change for me. Just as in the first session at the bookstore, I always saw myself as a child. For example, in my second past-life regression I saw myself as a ten-year-old living in medieval times in northern Europe, wearing brown, raglike clothing without any kind of footwear. This time, I went deeper and spent more time there. In that lifetime, I had an unusual ability to know of things to come. I somehow knew that the crops in the village would fail from drought, from pests, from too much rain and other catastrophes. When what I had predicted came true, my village needed someone or something to blame, and they picked me. I was sent to a primitive type of cell for foretelling those events, for speaking my truth. The cell, a simple wooden structure, had a dirt floor covered with straw and a metal door with slats. I couldn't reach the only small window built into one of its walls. I remained locked up in that cell until I was twelve years old.

Instead of spreading understanding, my gift had created fear, along with doubt in conventional religion. Since religion and authority (government) were connected at the hip during this time, it was as if I had thumbed my nose at both of those institutions. I was summarily rewarded with death, finally hung inside the cell like a side of beef.

I felt no pain or remorse. The common people couldn't have stopped my execution, for they had little power. Laws were made by and for the rich, the elite. The religious elders simply stood by and allowed the bloodletting, for they, too, thought that hanging me would help alleviate the devil's work. That is how they viewed prophecy coming from anyone who was not named in the Bible but who had the same powers as those who were described in the Bible. This unhappy ending for me just seemed to be a part of the natural cycle of life.

In my regressions, I was at times male and at others times female. Gender didn't matter, just as I don't think it matters to today's children. Whether I was male or female didn't seem to affect the way I thought or the way I acted. In addition, the first group of regressions I experienced were all during a period of time where there was little or no authority on the outskirts of towns, at least not in the towns I lived in.

Society's outcasts lived at the edge of town—the thieves, muggers and drunkards, along with all the nonsense that goes with that, men and women disassociated from love, and the castaway children. Anarchy ruled. We castaways were seen as unclean, and no one of importance wanted to be near us. They were too afraid of catching some horrible disease. It also seemed that children, especially unwanted children, were occasionally rounded up by a person or groups of people from the town, just as a dogcatcher or deputies of law would round up undesirables, and the city government received money from selling children. In some places, the abandoned orphans of a township were done away with to avoid the whole matter of feeding, clothing and caring for them.

Another regression opened yet another scene of death at an early age. A crowd of unhappy people, just outside a large town in the fifteenth century, stoned me to death. In this lifetime, I was a girl. My best friend had light hair and mine was brown. My friends and I were playing a game called "pretend" with a handful of our friends. Some of us were sitting while others stood along an embankment near a small wooden bridge. A group of malcontents, "uglies," as we called them, appeared out of nowhere and began pounding us with huge stones. We had no chance of escape. And then, like a whisper on the wind, my soul was carried to a different past.

As with the previous regressions, I saw myself in medieval times but could not read a calendar. This time I was a girl of about six or seven. Every so often, an ox-pulled wagon driven by one or two men and filled with children would pass by. I was part of a group of children who always ran to the back of the wagon to see if anyone we knew was inside. If so, we grabbed them, quickly pulled them off the wagon and hid them with us to save them from further harm. The children in that town were gathered up to be used as slaves, sold, added to other families or, at times, even eliminated. Sometimes it seemed to us that those alternatives were better than living in constant fear, surrounded by the "uglies."

Still, we were always ready to run and run fast. It was traumatic and frightening to be ripped from our homes, to be separated from our parents or brother or sister, to be sold into slavery or abandoned and left to fend for ourselves among the undesirables of society. As abandoned waifs, we were treated like animals that existed for the amusement of others. There was no one to take us in, no one to hold us, no one to care for us.

In the lives that were revealed to me through those early regression sessions, not only had I lived in disturbing times, but I never lived long enough to grow up. Only one of these first journeys into the past revealed that I had almost reached the ripe old age of twenty-one. In that life, I died in 1944 during World War II, just short of my twenty-first birthday, as I was getting out of one of the flattop boats landing on the shores of Normandy. I was pushed out of the boat along with the others in the rush and confusion and plain naked fear that abounded.

We had been packed in so tightly, shoulder to shoulder, front to back. Bullets were flying everywhere and the guy maneuvering the boat let the front armored door down long before reaching shore.

We were like rats escaping from a sinking ship. The water was far over my head and I couldn't get all of the heavy equipment off my back fast enough. Part of my clothing became entangled in some metal object under the water. At first I struggled relentlessly. My wild panic began to subside as exhaustion set in, as my life began to fade out. One last time I gasped, clawed for breath and pulled on the metal object that clung to the back of my clothing. Oxygen—sweet, loving oxygen—was far out of reach. As I slipped into acceptance, I saw a dim light. After a pause of what seemed an eternity, the light brightened and I felt as if I was in a body of fluid, moving into a birthing canal.

Although past-life regressions are emotional and can be stressful, when this regression ended I couldn't wait to dig deeper. But for now, I just wanted to relax and enjoy this moment of breath. To inhale so deeply and cleanly, to hold it for a few seconds and then to let it go slowly felt so refreshing. It's amazing how something so common as breathing in and out can change a moment, an attitude, a day, even the world.

The Mysterious Girl

Curt was skeptical about angels, the afterlife and what he referred to as ESP. To this intelligent twenty-three-year-old, who was attending college and working as a bank teller, these were all some kind of trickery. But recently he'd had an experience that had shaken him and he needed to tell someone about it. That someone happened to be me.

"It was a sunny day and I was at work at the bank," he told me. There are two entrances to Bank of America—the main entrance where the parking lot is and a door that goes out onto a road. I was working at the merchant teller station closest to the street-side entrance. I have close to one hundred grand at my station at times and even more around closing time.

"Out of the corner of my eye, I saw two or three guys jump out of a grey, eighties-style Cadillac and come in through the street-side door. They immediately surrounded me. I stayed calm and could see their every move coming, but I couldn't react. I was just frozen. I was so frightened that I couldn't lie on the ground like everyone else, as the robbers had ordered.

"One robber took out his gun and pointed it at me in almost a punching motion. The barrel was about an inch from my eyes. At that point, things seemed to evolve in slow motion as the robber pulled the trigger. I could see the bullet come out of the barrel. *Bang!* I woke up and let out a huge gruntlike scream as if I had the wind knocked out of me. That was the most startling dream I have ever had in my life." As it turned out, that was only the beginning of Curt's unusual night.

"At that point," he continued, "I was lying in the fetal position in bed. But after the bang, I found myself sitting up with my arms wrapped around my legs, knees to my chest, sweating and breathing hard.

"Just as I was sitting there, realizing it was all a dream, I saw something move at the foot of my bed. It was dark in the room, but I could see, standing at the end of my bed, a charming little girl. Her facial expression looked as if I had woken her and she had come to the room to see what the problem was. She had long hair. I couldn't tell if it was blond or brown, but it shone with the moonlight that came through the window. She was wearing a dress or nightgown or something like that, nothing flashy or too noticeable."

"How old was she?" I asked.

"Probably about seven years old, give or take a year or two," he said.

Trying to convince me that he hadn't made all this up, he added, "Look, I don't drink or do drugs. I stay clear of that stuff and always have."

"Then what happened?" I asked, assuring him that I understood.

"The little girl walked from the foot of the bed to my left side. She seemed totally real, no transparency, no translucency—just a real girl that had made her way into the room. I don't think I blinked at all, just watched in amusement. I wasn't scared or concerned, only curious about why she was there. I didn't say anything. I just followed her with my eyes.

"As she was standing right next to me, I broke eye contact with her momentarily, as if to test what I was encountering. I looked away, then back to her again. At that instant, she faded and was gone. I didn't understand how she could have been standing where she was, since right next to my bed, where I had seen her, was a nightstand and a dresser. Yet there she had stood."

Curt had obviously never delved into matters like this before. Now he was all curiosity, his words spilling out quickly. "She wasn't threatening or anything like that," he went on. "So what do you think? Was she an angel? She didn't have any wings."

"After hearing about your encounter," I said, "I would say the girl probably died years ago. I don't think she's an angel, at least not one of the winged ones. By the way, I don't doubt you at all, because you don't have anything to gain by telling a story like this. I do believe that what you experienced was real."

"She was just like you and me," Curt explained again. "I couldn't see through her."

"That's exactly the way some people see loved ones who have passed over. People who have had experiences like this tell me that they have conversations with their loved ones, just as you and I are talking with each other now. They see their sons, fathers, mothers, whoever it is, as clear as we are seeing each other. Those who have passed on don't always appear this way to the people who see them, but sometimes they do. So, just so know, you aren't alone."

Curt ran his hands through his hair and said he had no idea who this little girl was. I intuited (or rather, my angels told me) that she probably once lived in the house where Curt was now residing. I decided not to mention this to him since he had enough to digest for now.

I didn't see Curt until several months later, when he and a friend of his stopped by the store. He leaned over the counter and in a quiet voice, so his friend couldn't hear, said, "I found out that the family who first lived in the house where I'm staying right now had a little girl. She had an illness and died in her sleep there. That's why they moved out of the house and rent it now. Oh yeah, my bedroom used to be hers."

All I could do was smile back at him. He nodded, as if we were on the same page. Whether or not Curt now believes in the supernatural, I don't know. But I'm sure this meeting of flesh and spirit, of past and future, happened for a good reason, one that only Curt can figure out for himself.

CHAPTER FOURTEEN

The Aloha Spirit

It was a beautiful evening as we sat with John and Judy Peters in their backyard, talking, placing a log on the fire occasionally and gazing up at the wonderfully star-studded sky that God had placed above our heads. They had invited Pamela and me to their home in Cave Creek one cool Arizona evening in November for a home-cooked meal, conversation and a past-life regression.

I was eager to take advantage of Judy's offer, hoping I could go deeper still into my personal history, the history that stretched back much farther than just this lifetime. Past-life regressions, I knew, weren't for everyone. But for me, they were filling in some of the missing links in my soul's journey, helping me make sense of certain connections and conditions I had been dealing with in this life. Many times in my prayers and meditations I would ask the Great Source if I was still on the right path with the PLRs. I never got a negative response. I stayed the course, if for no other reason than self-assurance. I felt that through the experience of these regressions, I was receiving both spiritual and emotional healing.

Before we dined that night, we prayed for peace in the Middle East. The conversation was easy yet somewhat serious at times as we discussed the impending war with Iraq and the troubles in Afghanistan. After dinner, Judy asked, "Are you ready to step into the time machine?" I nodded and smiled. John and Pam went out back by the fire ring and I followed Judy to her study, where my journey into the past would begin. Thinking over my recent past-life regressions and the fact that I had attained adulthood only once, I had no expectations, only curiosity. But I did feel Spirit in the room, embracing us as we came together. I felt relaxed and, if anything, a little worried about falling asleep after the great meal and conversation.

The room was uncluttered and had a simple elegance to it. A majestic oak desk stood in the middle of the room with a matching chair behind it and a large, overstuffed brown leather chair in the front. There were two pictures on the wall. One was a beach scene showing children dispersing in every direction, the ebb and flow of the ocean, sailboats and a dog or two running about the shore. The other portrayed the snow-capped Canadian Rockies in a wintry mist.

Judy set me at ease immediately and began counting backwards. In between the counting, she told me to feel the various parts of my body relax and become heavy. It wasn't long before I was ready to see what lay behind this life.

When going through a regression, the therapist asks a number of questions to verify the time period, questions such as: Can you see a calendar? What type of clothing are you wearing? What type of footwear? What is your name? Are you male or female? Do you recognize anyone with you? What do you see around you? This time, I was in a fairly deep hypnotic state, so I don't recall much of the session. It's only through Judy's notes that I can tell you the following story.

I've always seen my past lives as if they were a movie. I see a series of film clips one after the other in rapid succession, not necessarily in linear, logical order. I don't know if my being left-handed and somewhat dyslexic has anything to do with the film clips being out of order, but that's the way the scenes appear to me. I've arranged them here in chronological order for better clarity for all you right-handed nondyslexics.

I began my recollections by seeing myself as a man of thirty, although in those days age wasn't the ultimate measure of one's life span. I lived in a long, rectangular green building with a pitched roof in a rain forest on top of a lush hilltop surrounded by water. I was barefoot, wearing anklets and bracelets made of braided reeds and flower stems, a hoop around my neck and a grass skirt for lower body cover. I lived with my wife, Ane. My name was, or sounded like, Patkahe. I knew I was on the island chain we now call Hawaii.

In retrospect, it makes sense that Hawaii has remained a dear and special place to me. My first connection with Hawaii started way back in 1959, when I attended my first luau in Lone Rock, a tiny town in Wisconsin, in the left field of a softball diamond. I was only ten at the time, but I remember that celebration of Hawaii becoming the fiftieth state of the union.

Although Judy asked me if I could see a calendar, I could not see one. In fact, I didn't know if this was happening in the future or near the beginning of mankind. In some ways, what I experienced felt the way the Garden of Eden has been described. We lived in an almost blissful state of mind in harmony with our surroundings.

"What do you see?" Judy asked. I described to her the hut I lived in. It had no windows and the thatched roof pitched down to within a few feet of the ground. A small, narrow furrow was dug along three sides of the hut, just below the drip line. It was filled with what I called "water stones," stones taken from mountain streams that had been worn smooth and rounded over time by the flowing waters. The water flowed from the rear entrance and poured into a series of three wells before it ran down the hill toward the aqua-blue ocean below.

When Judy asked me if I had seen anything unusual, I told her about a symbol that was carved in stone and used in rituals. All the people had that symbol carved out of wood in their homes. It seemed to be a powerful image that held deep meanings. The symbol wasn't anything weird or difficult to translate; it was a simple triangle with a wide bottom that symbolized a way of life, spiritually, emotionally and even mathematically. The people believed that the triangle held the key to all the mysteries of life.

No particular ruler or dictator was in charge or lording it over the masses of people on the island. There seemed to be simply a knowing of how to behave that created a smooth continuity among the various groups of people. If religion was practiced, it didn't seem to be the center point of life. We did have ceremonies and rituals to give thanks to the life that sustained our lives—to our sacred earth, blessed sky, fruit trees, mountains streams, the ocean and other living things, such as plants and animals.

"Did anything unusual happen while you were there?" Judy asked. I shared with her that a monumental event had taken place while I was there. One day, daylight became darkness, yet in the darkness it was still very bright. There were lights in the sky that looked like the floodlights used today for grand openings and movies, except that these lights were multicolored. Hues of yellows and oranges, greens and blues flashed about in a loose pattern, moving from east to west, north to south. Everyone scurried back to their huts, peering at the sky from the safety of their homes. My wife and I ran from one end of the house to the other, following the movement of the lights, feeling bewildered, excited and fearful. We had never seen anything like this before. We were transfixed by the spectacle.

Large, narrow crystalline tubes began forming in the sky around the island, causing a swirling and spraying directly below in the ocean. The spiraling waters rose up to a point where they met the tubes, which pushed the water back down. Inside and outside, the crystalline tubes were illuminated with hues of rainbows. An electric and magnetic force surrounded the tubes. As the tubes plunged down into the water, the skies above the tubes swirled with colorful hues and static electricity in the opposite direction of the swirling waters below.

From the top of the brilliantly lit tubes flowed what appeared to be energies of great knowledge that were being fed into life forms, accompanied by tremendous humming sounds of static electricity. The life forms looked more like the Pillsbury doughboy than anything else I can relate to, except they were transparent and ran the whole gamut of the color spectrum. As the energies of great knowledge entered these life forms, they became brighter and brighter. The light and the life forms became one. These light/life forms of color came through the tubes in a narrow beam, landing softly on the chest of all the people of the island. This didn't hurt, but when the colorful light forms made contact with us, something entered our bodies in the form of knowledge and imbedded itself into the very fiber of our beings.

I received immediate knowledge about the various colors that now radiated from within our bodies and glowed outwardly from us. Each color held a particular significance and related to molecules of pigmentation. These molecules were being placed within us for future use. We were the children of God and it was through us that the various "colors" of the people of the world would evolve.

In later generations, as our knowledge of traveling by boat from island to island was enhanced, we would be the ones who set sail to various parts of the world. At one time, we all had brown eyes, but as we populated other parts of the world, the color of our eyes would begin to change. It would happen over time, from generation to generation. Some would be born with blue eyes or green eyes or hazel eyes. From that life-changing encounter of the crystalline tubes on this remote island, a shift of grand proportions was begun and it would eventually encompass the entire world.

At this point in the regression, because of the spectacular event taking place from out of the sky, I could not make out if I was living in the past or the future. I felt confused as to whether I had gone back in time or forward into the future for a pre-life preview.

As Patkahe, I felt my heart begin racing. It was pounding hard for quite a while. Then the pounding began to soften and my heartbeat became irregular. Eventually, the heartbeat faded and ceased altogether. Ane held my hand as I lay on the cool moist grass next to the house. I remember her kissing my cheek as a beam of light entered my eyes. It held my attention and I felt my body become light as it floated up and toward the beautiful, loving white light.

"Where did you go?" Judy asked gently. I told her I was in the light, or I was light—a photon, a ray, carrying the frequency of a beam, able to transform into any color vibration associated with an emotional feeling. I was moving above the island so high that I could see water all around. I had never seen anything like this before. I felt sad that I could not see my wife or my home. The light comforted me during this transitional phase. As time went on, I felt more and more at home in the light.

The color of the light I had become changed many times. I could see nothing outside of phosphorescence. I didn't feel human or like anything made of matter. I was far beyond any universe, or had I even begun my journey? I had no feeling. A far-off light was calling, yet I didn't know where to go. The symbol of the triangle was luring me, but this time the triangle didn't have a wide base. It looked more like a steeple than a pyramid.

I was engulfed by the sensation of floating as I felt myself going into a churchlike building. I didn't feel comfortable there. I realized I was in a body again. I wasn't made of light, although light was still inside of me. At least it felt that way. I was in a body of a newborn child and I was growing quickly. I felt as if I were a child playing, but I did not feel complete—something was not quite right with me. Coping with my surroundings was a real chore.

I saw colors of green and brown and a mass of water on the ground. I saw myself as a child, a white spirit person who was neither male nor female. I felt incomplete, in limbo—in between spirit and human form. I was looking at myself looking back at me. I saw myself dressed in loose-fitting clothing. There was laughter and peacefulness on the island. Then I was set down from up above, yet I felt partly there and partly not. I was not ready to touch down, not ready to come back.

I was beginning to feel uncomfortable and was almost panicking when I said out loud, "Not yet ready! It did not happen, back to nothingness, back up the plasma tubes again and the white light. Walk me there. I can go there."

"It is not your time," said Judy. "Go to a place where you lived a long life and where life was lived well; hence, death was not something to fear but part and parcel to life itself."

Next stop, the Holy Land.

Prophetic Dreams

Glenda, an elderly woman with glasses and a lavender scarf around her head, came over to the counter where I was working, put her shopping bag down and opened up to me. She was straightforward and very intent on telling me her story.

Glenda had been living alone for many years. "My children and grandchildren live in different states," she explained. "My husband and I had been separated and then divorced for over twenty years, but we remained friends. Five years ago, he had a heart attack and died. As a family, we didn't practice a particular religion, but I believed in God, although my husband didn't.

"In my later years, I wanted to know more about the spiritual world and I asked God for guidance, assuring him that I was open and ready for spiritual intervention in my life. I prayed hard for two years and nothing happened. Then I surrendered my thoughts to God and said, 'I know this will happen according to your will and time, not mine.' Then I let it go. For a while, I was fairly content with life, but then the dreams started coming."

Glenda paused. When she began again, her voice was trembling and she looked directly into my eyes. "You're the first person I've told about this," she said. "I've been afraid to tell anyone else!" I encouraged her to go on and tell me about her dreams.

"For several years now, I have been receiving dreams," she explained. "In my dreams, I see good things that are going to happen and I see tragedies. Sometimes I see plane crashes three days before they take place. I see the faces and terror of everyone on the plane just before it disintegrates with fire and explosion. Immediately following the crash, I see the people in spirit form going up into the sky, floating toward heaven. But not all of them. Some stay by the crash site and others sort of flutter about as if they are lost. I feel terrible! I'm afraid that people will think I'm crazy or make me feel bad about not notifying someone when I get those dreams. I don't see what flight they are on, though, and the planes are almost always from countries other than America. I just feel so guilty and afraid right now."

Tears flowed down Glenda's cheeks. She shuddered. I handed her a box of tissues as I came around the counter and stood next to her. I shared something a nun I had known once told me. When I had asked the nun why the bishop, priests and others did some of the nasty things they did, she replied, "When you want to see something up close, sometimes you get to see it, warts and all."

Glenda grabbed more tissues, trying to collect herself. "Here's what happened just recently," she continued tearfully. "An acquaintance of mine who works in the same building where I work was in a car accident. I saw it before it happened, but I didn't know how to approach her about it because she flat out refused to listen to me whenever I brought up the subject of spirituality or the afterlife.

"In my dream, I saw her driving at night through her neighborhood on a short trip that she needn't have taken, and her car was struck by another on the driver's side. I tried desperately during the next couple of days to talk to her. I wanted to stop it from happening by making plans with her to go out to eat after work, to go shopping, to do anything, but she always had an excuse for leaving that evening open just for herself. She wasn't doing anything special that evening, yet she didn't want to be bothered to go out with me. Her car was broadsided at an intersection just a block from where she lived by someone in a stolen car. She was killed immediately."

Glenda trembled through most of this part. I opened my arms and we hugged until she regained her composure.

"I know you feel as if there is nothing you can do," I whispered to Glenda. "But you can pray. You can turn over whatever you see to God, to the universe, to the light. You can ask God to send angels to intercede to stop the terrible tragedies if at all possible. But we can't stop fate. If it is one's turn to leave here and go to the light, so be it. Maybe somehow, some way, some events can be delayed, but when it's our time to go, it will happen. It's not possible to change all things."

Out came the tissue box again. "You can do one more thing for those leaving," I added. "You can tell the spirit to go to the light or call upon Michael archangel to help those who die suddenly or violently to go to the light. You can also ask that all of their pain and suffering be forgotten in all ways and in all time."

"Since the dreams started, I've been writing them down," Glenda said in between sniffs. She shook her head back to regain her composure and took a deep breath. "Now, I have to tell you something else," she said. "I have to tell you about my granddaughter."

Glenda's face lightened up. "I have three lovely granddaughters and I love them dearly," she said. "There is one I rarely get to see since my daughter and I don't see eye to eye on some things. She always has an excuse as to why I can never come to visit. I wish she would lighten up a little. She is so rigid, especially with her religion! They won't accept me now, knowing that I have been awakened to Spirit through my dreams.

"I miss having contact with my little five-year-old granddaughter, Brittany, but she does call me almost every day and she tells me what she sees. For instance, she tells me that she sees her grandfather (my late husband) at family functions or on the playground. Brittany was only seven months old when he died. There's no way she could know who he is! They don't even have a picture of him in their house."

One day, Glenda asked Brittany if she understood the word *telepathy*. "Yes, Grandma," the little girl said, "I understand the meaning better than you do." "I was surprised," said Glenda, "but I believed her, because I know that that word and anything like it has never been used in her house. My daughter and her husband don't believe in any of that. And then during one of our precious phone conversations, Brittany told me that I would be going shopping the following Saturday with three or four friends. I did have a shopping trip planned for Saturday, but there was just no way Brittany could have known. She lived far away in another state and I'd never said a word to her about it."

"One other thing," Glenda added toward the end of our conversation. "Brittany also told me that she was an angel before she was born. In fact, she told me that at one time, she was an angel of mine, an angel who was supposed to help me! Brittany said that the angels she knew worked in groups. In her group, there happened to be seventy adult angels and one other young girl who was her age—seventy-two angels in all."

After hearing Glenda unfold her story, I realized that Brittany could well be one of the new generation of children who are being born now, the "crystal children." Crystal children are powerful and loving and they are here to help all of us heal and evolve spiritually. They are extremely sensitive and have innate spiritual gifts, especially telepathic abilities.

Brittany, may you walk always with angels and help us do so too. And may God help you, Glenda, to be strong and to fulfill your deepest spiritual desires. When you see life end swiftly, ask the spirit to go to the light or ask for the help of God's angels to guide that one toward the light, the light of eternal bliss and love.

CHAPTER FIFTEEN

The Mission of Love

By following the lead of the angels, I was learning more about myself than I had ever thought possible. Of course, there is no way to prove that the information that came to me or that comes to any of us through past-life regressions is totally accurate—not yet anyway. Far more important is what we *do* with the information we receive. Are we using what's revealed to us as a springboard to grow more and to love more? In the long history of our souls, we have all, at one time or another, been among the paupers and the princes, the simple folk and illustrious ones. It's not who we *were* that's important, but who we are learning to become. Learning about past lives was helping me understand more about the archetypal journey of every soul and the lessons all of us have come here to learn.

The regressions were awe-inspiring events that communicated to me the love that is within us and around us, and they affirmed what I learned in my dream, the one that allowed me that incredible peek into heaven. All the regressions I experienced, especially the ones with Judy, helped me remember who I am and put me on a wonderful path leading back to me. I now feel content to be who I am, and I love me. What I've seen and felt in my regressions, especially the second one with Judy, even challenged some popular misconceptions about what took place centuries and millennia ago.

So far, my session with Judy had affirmed my connection with Hawaii. As we continued, I received yet another affirmation. A number of years ago, in an angel reading I received over the phone, a woman in Oregon told me that a powerful, spiritual male energy force was with me. She went on to say that it was Lazarus, the dear friend of Jesus. She said that Lazarus was my "spirit guide," that he had been my father in another lifetime and that he was with me to guide me to the truth. My past-life regression with Judy not only confirmed her message, but it also unfolded a much larger story.

"Okay, now back," I heard myself saying aloud in a childlike voice, as Judy helped me move to another time and place. "I am now in a place with people, buildings, big birds and other animals. It is good. I know of no mother at my house. My older sisters were mothers to me. My father is sick. I am a small child, maybe three years old. I have sisters who are much older than I. There is a feeling of light around our house and our hearts, a love-light like the presence of Yeshua, as though God is close. I play there. Yeshua is near. He talks to my father and jokes with my sisters when he comes."

"Describe what you see and hear," Judy directed.

"Animals, donkeys, sheep, chickens are nearby," I responded. "Men with long sticks are pushing the sheep, and there are donkeys in a pen below our house. They make funny noises. We have chickens, but I am afraid of the roosters. They chase me and I cry. Our family has many visitors and we enjoy having them here and listening to their stories. The food is bread and soup for me. The bread is round and dark and hard for me to chew. It looks funny to me. The soup is good when there is food from our garden in it. There is much soil with few trees. Lots of rocks. I play with rocks. I line them up in formations around the yard. Sometimes I try to give weeds to the donkeys as they stand near our house.

"What are the names of those nearby?"

"Sara—she's nice. Marwee [Mary], Roof Zackual, Zeke, Zake." I am too young to pronounce words or names correctly.

"Speak as an adult and tell me of the times when Jesus would visit," Judy encouraged.

"You say 'Jesus,' but his name was Yeshua," I said. "He often came to visit. I remember him being called 'The Light.' When he spoke with my father and the rest of the family, he was a force of gaiety to be around. There was a happy, calm peace that rang throughout our home.

"I played at his knee, around and underneath the chair he sat in. I climbed on him and he picked me up, lifting me upwards to the sky and back down. I remember his big wide smile and warm touch. He was so loving, so very alive. I could almost feel the energy within him. His arms and hands were warm, almost hot. Being touched by him felt like an embrace. He was a young man with olive-colored skin—like mine, only lighter—and he had brown, wavy hair down to his shoulders and a soft, short, pointed beard.

"The Light talks of sailing far away with his uncle Joseph,

two of Joseph's sons and other cousins. They visited many lands and met people with many differences and different languages. He told of sailing a long distance on rough seas to islands of enchantment and also of walking and riding camels into far-off deserts when he was younger.

"The Light was animated and told many stories. He visited more often when I was a toddler. The last visit was during a traumatic time at home. My father had been ailing for quite some time. Sadness filled our family and much agitation filled the minds of the adults. There were many visitors in the house, who were told my father was in a coma. Eventually, his breathing stopped. I did not understand that. My older sisters were crying and that made me anxious, causing me to whine and whimper.

The Light arrived, followed by many, many people, who stayed at a distance from our house as he entered. His face was not the happy face I was accustomed to, and his mood was solemn. There was no laughing this time. He went with Mary, my older sister (Mary Magdalene), into the room where my father had been sleeping for days. When they reappeared, my father followed them out of the room. There was much commotion and Yeshua left the house with Mary at his side.

"Move ahead ten years or to a time you can remember and tell me how old you are," said Judy.

"I am fifteen. My father, Lazarus, died years earlier. When Yeshua left after healing my father, my favorite older sister, Mary, the one who spent time with me, caring for me and playing with me, left with him. She went with a group of men and women to tell others in neighboring villages and far-away places about the ways of Yeshua. Mary came back after many long months of travel. She was a changed person.

"No longer happy, she was angry with the men. She felt betrayed by them and Yeshua's brother James, who was with the group. James had changed the teachings that Yeshua proclaimed as Truth. Yeshua had taught of women being equal to men and superior in ways that men could not be. James did not like that, and he and another leader of her group urged the others to rid the rest of the group of the women. She began the task of writing. I don't recall all she wrote, but she never quit writing. She wrote during the day and far into the night of what Jesus had taught her. She seldom smiled again.

"I am with others now. Some are my age and others are older. We have had to leave our homes and walk. I am angry and confused. The foreign armies have been aggressive toward some of my people and that is why we are on the move.

"Yeshua, the Light, was put to death not long after awakening my father. Some said it was the wishes of the priests and elders of our people, yet we had no death penalty. Yeshua could do no harm to warrant such a cruel fate.

"My group consists of cousins, a friend of mine from the area near my house and two younger distant female cousins of Yeshua. We are certain that it was the foreigners who tricked some into believing that he was a criminal for teaching our beliefs in a way that was more open than the overly stern elders and priests permit. But even then, we would not put our own to death!

"It is very strange and I am angry over this. We the Jewish people are divided in thought. I refuse to learn and I don't want the teachings of the old ways. Yeshua taught of many different people in the world and said that they, too, must know God. Our priests and elders say, 'Our way is the only way to God's kingdom; let them find their own gods.' They ridicule the non-Jews, the Gentiles, for the way they worship things, including trees. I go with others who knew Yeshua and who follow his thought. Food is hard to come by. We go to another place of learning. We come upon groups of people of our faith and language. We listen to them and we speak our truth.

"We walk great distances with pack animals and carry as much food as possible with water and sometimes wine. I like the sensations of wine swishing in my mouth and running down over my tongue. We do not leave our country yet. We see people who talk strangely and who pray in circles with heads bowed to the ground. They are not of our faith and people. We talk of a new way, the Way of Yeshua's teachings. People listen to us as we speak with words of love for our faith, as they do of theirs. Yet our teaching is different because we teach what Yeshua taught: *"Allow our Mother-Father God and way of life to be universal so all who live in our land and nearby can feel the warmth, the light and the love. Make it inclusive, not exclusive."*

"Some of the older ones with my group remember Yeshua talking of a nurturing, kind and loving God. He never talked of a God who held grudges or ruled that one was better or worse than another. Yeshua called God 'the Mother-Father God.' He said that God knows both ways, the way of woman as well as the way of man. To know them both allows one to be with God forevermore.

"People have a difficult time with even minor changes or new thought. As we travel, we see so many people who are not like us. They do not look like us, talk like us or worship as we do. They look like lost sheep and, as Yeshua was heard to say, 'God is with them too. They need to know God as much as we need to know God.' He said they are our brothers and sisters, yet that is hard for us to understand.

"For the most part, the foreign soldiers (Romans) do not know our language. They may own us now, but in time we know our land will once again belong to us. We make jokes about them as we pass by, and then try to keep from laughing until we are at a safe distance. The soldiers do not harm us. We do not carry weapons. They do not interfere with us unless we provoke them, or they are drunk. Then maybe...."

"Any more about Jesus?" Judy asked.

"I do not remember his specific teachings much, because I was so young when he was around, but those in my family say he spoke of love as if it were a healing device. I definitely felt his presence. The ones who were with him told us of his teachings as well. I could never forget his larger message. He said: *Love is really what God intended life to be about. Unconditional love is a connection to God—one true love as a rainbow, the beginning and the end, the Alpha and the Omega.*" Yeshua spoke of Moses and indicated that Moses had been here more than once. There is confusion about that among the elders.

"Although I am old now, I go with my group to help others know of the gentle teachings of Yeshua ben-Joseph. I am getting frail and cannot continue. I lay on the desert floor. I have a vision of my oldest sister coming for me, although she died years earlier. It is odd to me. She is glowing and reaches for my hand and I rise up, remembering the words of Yeshua: *Watch carefully of words that cause heartache and cause division. If we do not use them, they can do no harm nor cause confusion. By using them, we think them aloud and breathe harm into life, and this causes much destruction. Remove those thoughts from your hearts and the words from your memory and they will not be. Eliminate wasteful thought and there shall be peace and hearts filled with love, for it is in the heart that God resides."* Yeshua also taught: *"God lives for us all, as I have lived for you."*

"Where are you going now?" asked Judy.

"To the light, in the light. Moving fast, back to the Islands, I think to the time when it all started: rainbows, beaches, serenity, peaceful bliss, a warmth and feeling of being at home. I see a man of great dignity and power. People bow and listen. He is a large man with brown skin and a person with much authority, yet he is humble. He gives knowledge to those who come to him for insight."

"Do you want to continue?"

"I'm growing tired."

"I will bring you back now."

Following the past-life regression with Judy, my strength was spent. The complexity of the readings, yet the paradoxical ease with which time flowed, brought a sense of immense bliss. A deep feeling of serenity engulfed me. I felt authentic, pure, if you will, and that night I slept like a baby.

Archangel Michael's Healing Touch

Karina was staying with a close friend in Mesa, Arizona, who directed her to Angel Wings. They came in to look for angels and, in particular, a likeness of Michael, the archangel. Karina was also looking for some answers. She wanted to talk about an experience she had had, one she couldn't talk about with her relatives. Like her friend, Karina was in her mid-twenties. She had coal-black hair and beautiful dark eyes. She spoke Spanish and, with the help of her friend, did her best to tell me her story.

Just a few days earlier, she had been praying for her seven-year-old nephew, Christopher, who was lying in a hospital bed in a coma. Christopher and his aunt had been in a car accident. The little guy had hit his head hard and, with a swollen brain, was in a coma. The doctors told the family that he might have many hurdles to overcome as a result of the injury. As she sat next to Christopher's father in the hospital room, she closed her eyes and bowed her head, praying for her nephew's well-being and recovery.

Karina finished her prayers, opened her eyes and looked toward Christopher, bewildered and in disbelief at what she was seeing. Hovering directly above Christopher, with one hand on his face and one on his head, was a beautiful angel. He was over seven feet tall with golden flowing hair and a brilliant, copper-colored face that appeared strong yet peaceful. She said the angel had a healing presence to him, that he was wearing a tunic of bright blue with some gold that stopped just above his knees and that his sandals laced up around his calf muscles. An aura of cobalt blue sparkled around the angel and he was adorned with shimmering silver wings.

Karina turned to Christopher's father to awaken him so that he could see what she was witnessing, but he was sleeping, his head bent down and his chin resting on his chest. Her nudging failed to waken him. Karina turned her attention back to her nephew. The angel was still there. She watched as the angel, smiling and looking down on Christopher, his arms still extended toward the child's head, floated upward toward and then through the ceiling. Then he disappeared. Stunned, Karina didn't want to say anything about what she had seen to Christopher's father or to anyone else.

The next day, after work, Karina returned to the hospital. Once more, she found herself in the room with the boy's father and she closed her eyes and bowed her head in prayer. At the conclusion of her prayers, she lifted her head and opened her eyes. This time, she saw what she described as two angels surrounding Christopher, but, to her surprise, they had no wings.

One of these "angels," the one directly over Christopher, was rather short. As Karina paused in her telling of this story, I received an intuitive feeling about who it was. I told her it was Christopher's grandfather, who had passed on earlier. She thought about that for a while, and then nodded her head, saying she remembered that his grandfather had passed over years before and the spirit above the child's head fit his grandfather to a tee.

"But who was that other funny little man who was with him?" she asked. She described the second being as just four feet tall and said he wore a shimmering white gown with gold around the neck and sleeves. His face was shaped like an oval, he was bald and he had a long cone-shaped white goatee six inches long that he stroked when he laughed, which he did, often. Karina giggled as she thought about him. He was so impish and made light of things around him.

"Maybe that was exactly that man's intention," I said, smiling. Many times, we take things so seriously, even though the situation is out of our hands. We simply forget to give our concern to the Lord and let the God-realm take it. That little man's actions may simply have been a reminder to you to let go of the situation and let God deal with it. Whatever or who-ever he was, take it as a special gift given to you by God." Karina went on to say that both figures hovered above her nephew, cradling his head in their hands in a comforting, healing way, as the archangel had done. She turned to her nephew's father, but again he was asleep. She looked back to the beings above Christopher's head and, like the radiant angel of the day before, they floated up through the ceiling and gently disappeared.

Karina and her friend had come into Angel Wings in hopes of under-standing and affirming these recent visions and of finding out who those little "angels" were. Her description of the first angel in blue sounded like Archangel Michael, so I pulled out Dr. Virtue's recent book on angels and ascended masters and read her its description of Michael. Upon hearing what Michael looked like and the colors associated with him, Karina's hand flew to her mouth and she gasped, "That is who I thought it was!"

With her new knowledge of Michael and her curiosity about the two other figures satisfied, Karina was more at peace with the events that had unfolded in her young life over the previous days. I never saw her again and

I don't what happened to her little nephew, but with angels and friends like these, I know he's in good hands.

Chapter Sixteen

Enjoying the Ride

It's all Pamela's fault, you know. It's Pamela who got me
thinking about angels. She started out collecting Santa Clauses,
all kinds of them. For a while she was on a kick to get a Santa
from every corner of the world. She got very close. For some
unknown reason, she shifted her attention to collecting angels—
angel ornaments, angel figurines, angel statuary.

Then I bought Pamela a book about angels for her birthday
and ended up reading it first. It came just at the right time. After
reading that book, and then the other books on angels that I
voraciously devoured, I wondered why the religion I had been
baptized into as an infant rarely spoke of angels. Although
organized religion seldom discusses angels, it does talk about us,
the churchgoers, as lowly beings, about the sins we commit and
about how difficult it is to reach heaven's gate. I'd been told by
priests that the Bible mentions only seven angels, but through a
conscious effort to find out more, I discovered that there are
many of them. In fact, there are groups of angels and they hold

various positions and lend themselves to diverse tasks. They are all a product of God's love, and they always answer our questions.

Among the many questions I started asking the angels was why religion seemed to be so complicated, why it often hurt the very ones who wanted to know more about it. Of course, one of the sacrificial lambs I was thinking about was the student body of the Holy Name seminary class of 1995 in Madison, Wisconsin. I was thinking about the bishop who called my son and his class an embarrassment to the Catholic Church. I don't blame Catholicism or any other religion for incidents like these that seem to ostracize those who are most dedicated to the Spirit. It's happened throughout the generations of organized religion. I see now that, in a way, this painful situation kickstarted my journey. Without it, I wouldn't be where I am today; for if it's a spiritual journey we crave, then our trek through life, with all of its joys and all of its obstacles, becomes food for the soul.

With angels on the scene, my anger and confusion about what I was seeing around me turned into intense curiosity. Searching for the truth became my all-consuming goal. I felt as if I were standing on the one-yard line with a ball tucked under my arm and the truth was far away at the other end of a 100-yard football field. The end zone was reachable, but the ground between was filled with uniformed, helmut-wearing obstacles—people positioned between that line and me. I had to confront and elude each one as I ran and zigzagged my way down the field toward the goal line. Funny thing, though, as I look back at those who were in front of me, trying to keep me away from that hallowed ground beyond the goal line, the faces of the obstacles looked a lot like me.

The angels became my best friends. They opened my eyes to new ways of looking at life, at my life in particular, and at the goal line. It was the angels who put me on a spiritual path that has been more like a beautiful ride through a cool starlit sky into previously unknown territory. The ride has taken hairpin turns and ups and downs that became peaks and valleys. But I wouldn't change it for the world.

The angels always point us in the right direction, even when we don't realize that they are here. It was those pesky little angels, I came to realize, who had been nudging me all along. They were the ones who guided me to find that angel book in the first place. Pamela's angel was the one who woke me up on a Monday morning in answer to her little prayer. It was angels who led us to a home on Crossroads Drive and to the angel store that would one day be our own. The winged ones also led me to Dr. Virtue's Angel Therapy Practitioner course and to past-life regressions, which affirmed the teachings of the universal Jesus on unconditional love and introduced me to the rainbow children of the place we now call Hawaii, a place where the past, present and future interact and play.

The angels helped me pierce the veil between heaven and earth, allowing me a look into heaven without needing to go through a near-death experience. Through my angel readings, they introduced me to ascended masters like Kuan Yin, Buddha, Krishna and others, as well as to spirit guides. I believe it was the angels who presented to me those dreams that were so significant, starting with that incredible peek into heaven and then the visions of people I would soon be meeting. The excitement, love and compassion I found in my first dream while I was in the presence of my teacher, Eddy, witnessing a higher learning, a higher realm, God's realm, makes me want to close my eyes and breathe deeply. It makes me yearn for the overwhelming love I felt in that place we call heaven.

Lessons learned from Edythe Carroll as she transitioned to the great ballroom in the sky touched my soul and kept me alert to the new beginnings of my own spiritual path to freedom. It was through Edythe that my buddy Lucille entered my life, albeit briefly. Her beautiful, loving and humorous spirit still makes me pause and smile in her direction. The lady in lavender, who appeared in my dream the morning Pamela and I flew to Hawaii in search of a place to open a store, was a sign of things to come. Seeing her in a little courtyard off that main street in Maui, where she unexpectedly told us she believed in angels too, was a prophecy that we would one day open our own angel store in a courtyard off a main street.

The angels guide my angel readings and they guide the people who come for help, assurance and comfort. They were also the ones who led me to work with hospice. The little daily miracles that came through the hospice experience quickly became life-changing events that opened my eyes to the power of Spirit. The *"Why me?"* questions eventually subsided and turned to affirmations of humbling gratitude: *"Thank you, Lord, for allowing visions and miracles to come my way."*

The miracles are no less, and no less frequent, at Angel Wings. I'm just a stranger to those who stop by the store and share their closely held secrets of spiritual encounters. I have come to know about archangels and guardian angels not just through books and angel readings, but also through the candid stories of these visitors, some of which I've shared in this book.

The angels have also helped me gain a deep love and respect

for a missing element in our Western traditions and culture—woman. From the time we are born, we are thrust into a new beginning, away from the warm nurturing and the loving womb of our mother. We begin a long journey away from her friendly confines to exposure to the outer world. When we find ourselves in search of food to sustain us, we find it in the breast of the one who brought us life.

Who is this person who cares for us, tends to our needs, protects us from the outer environs and gives us unconditional love? Woman. How is it that mankind exists and how did we arrive on this planet? Through woman. My journey has shown me that before God became a "he" in the scriptures and traditions that were handed down to us, God was both masculine and feminine. The Great Spirit was referred to as the Mother-Father God. What is the Mother-Father God? Whole, complete, universal, unconditional love. We have much to learn from woman. We have much to learn from God and from listening to the angels.

In the blessed presence of a quick moment in time where there is no thought, there is silence. That is where we find God, Spirit and spirituality. With the ever-increasing pace of our lives, it's more important than ever to take time to contemplate silence, to hear the voice of God, to feel the presence of the angels, to gravitate to our higher self and to distance ourselves from the lower self, the ego. Ego does not want you to change. It does not want quiet solitude or peaceful serenity. Ego wants status quo. It doesn't want you to move your life forward. Ego is not comfortable without chaos, without immediate highs and lows, anger and resentment.

Since working with the angels, I find myself spending more and more time with my higher self and less time with my ego. Though ego can raise its ugly head from time to time, I can now see it, feel it and hear it more quickly, and I use the tools I have learned to put it back down and away from my thought. I've learned to look more to my higher self to answer the big and important questions I have.

I've learned that we can take the leap beyond the ego and into the unknown when we let go of judgment, follow our hearts and listen to the angels. And I've learned that the journey is not about achieving goals or winning the game. The word *angel* literally means "messenger," and the angels' message is a simple one: *love.* That is what God is and that is what the journey is about. God (our Higher Source, our Inner Knowing, or whatever terminology you prefer) is love, complete unconditional love that leaves no room for anything else—no anger, no pain, no hatred, no judgment. When a child colors a picture and goes outside the lines, his parents love that picture anyway and tape it to the refrigerator door. That is what God's love is like. It doesn't matter that we step outside the boundaries or the lines; we are still loved.

Somewhere along the line, the simple teachings of love have been lost. "Do unto others as you would have them do unto you." "Love thy neighbor." Those basic teachings say it all, and they have roots that go much farther back in the past than just two thousand years. Are they too simple or too easy to take seriously?

Living in our higher self and letting go of ego is ultimately up to us. As a Hopi teaching says, *we are the ones we have been waiting for.* We can make this world a kinder and gentler place for all living creatures or we can choose not to. Although there is much darkness right now, the angels tell us of a more loving way to live and a better place to be.

Where is that place? Not far away really. Just pause, take a deep huna breath—a Hawaiian breath—smile as you do so and look inward. This will get you quickly to that place of peaceful bliss, the place where God resides within us. God is everywhere, but love starts with us. When we look inward, the search that has taken us far and wide comes to an end. The answers, we discover, are in our heart.

Things that I once thought were impossible are not only possible but are happening all the time. More and more people tell me of spiritual phenomena that are happening in their lives. People are speaking of their experiences more openly, without fear, and the angels are saying, "You go, girl!" "Atta boy, tell it like it is!" It is time to speak out and not to be afraid. Shout it from the rooftops: "We are not alone. The Spirit world is not in a distant galaxy. Heaven is not a place. It is all around us."

Whether you are battling debilitating hardships, terminal illness, emotional traumas or life's day-to-day challenges, remember that you are never alone, nor are you far away from God's healing love. Do not be afraid to call upon your guardian angels, archangels, Yeshua, Mary, God, or whomever you perceive as deity. Call upon them any time. They will come.

Take a cue from the angels and begin to look inward. Start with a simple step. Walk to the nearest bookstore and find a spiritual or inspirational book that catches your eye, or find a workshop or seminar that grabs your attention. Go to another and another until you find yourself removing ego altogether and you begin to live in your higher self, your God-self, in harmony and at peace with your surroundings. After all, isn't that what God wants—and isn't that why God sends his angels to us as messengers? So buckle up, sit back and enjoy the ride. Embrace the inner spiritual journey with your whole heart and soul.

CHAPTER SEVENTEEN

Prayers from the Heart

Prayers can work miracles, both for those who need them and for those who make them on behalf of others. At Angel Wings, resting on a table next to the front wall, surrounded by original paintings of angels, sits a special white porcelain prayer bowl. Next to the bowl is a sign that reads: *All the prayers asked for here are prayed for within twenty-four hours.* Every day, Pamela or I pray not only for the intentions placed in the bowl, but also for those who wrote the prayers. We ask that God's healing love touch each and every one who intercedes for a friend or loved one.

On the following pages, I've included some of the prayers that adults and children of all ages and backgrounds have dropped into our bowl with a special prayer in their hearts and on their lips. Feel free to add your own heart's desire to these intentions by repeating these prayers on behalf of those who need them or by making the same or a similar prayer for someone you know who is in need of angelic assistance or a miracle or two.

I also invite you to consider creating a special space in your home for your own unique prayer bowl. Write down your prayers to the angels, your questions and your deepest yearnings and place them in the bowl. The angels are always ready to listen, to act and to create miracles when you are least expecting it. They will never lie, for they are an extension of God's love. Just listen with your heart and you will hear their answers.

I pray for peace. Brianna

My name is Joanne. I would like my angels to guide me to do great paintings that can help heal people.

That we may pass on the joy and love we know.

I request to be clearly shown where I need to live—to feel much more fulfilled, content, joyful and at peace. Right now I just don't know, nor do I know how to get there. Thank you.

Please give me one day without pain. Anne

Help me at work, my boss doesn't like me.

Please keep Tim safe in Iraq.

Please help me find what was lost and guide me to it. Charlotta

That someday there may be total peace within our family and I can be free from depression. Thank you!

Note: The names have been changed in these prayer offerings.

Grant Paula peace as she passes on. Please grant Hanna under-standing as she continues.

Merciful Father, pray for Brenda and the loss of her son Lonny. Be with her and ease her pain and suffering and all who are grieving. Amen.

Please sell my house in 10 days.

Please, God, let Diane, Deborah and my Dad all be together in heaven.

For Darryl and Rita, for health and happiness. He has Crohn's disease and is not dealing with it. It is destroying their lives.

For my sons, Roger and Donny, that they find their angels. Toni

Help all the animals of the world. Caroline

For gene implant to be effective for battle with Alzheimer's.

Courage to do the right thing... Alicia

Josie would like and desire very much to find a life partner full of love and devotion. Love to God and my angels.

Please pray for my son James, age 26. He committed suicide this past Monday. He left a brief note saying that he asked God to for-give his sins and that he hoped we all would as well. He was loved, very loving, a humorous and a wonderful man, and none of us knew he was in such deep pain. Thank you.

A successful kidney transplant for my brother from myself. Pray for us.

For Ashley, for strength, confidence and whatever else she needs to make it through this semester. God bless this store, you are special! To find ourselves and purpose in life. For our enemies and those whose lives are filled with hatred, that spirit will touch their hearts.

Please help me play a good round of golf on Friday and be on a winning team. Thank you. Leanne

Roger L., a vet, needs many prayers mentally, physically, spiritually.

Help with drinking problem. Janice

Our baby, Kimberly, was 9½ months old, passed on January 14 of this year.

Pray for John, who recently had a liver transplant.

Wrap friends and family, especially Thomas, in an angel bubble.

For our son and daughter-in-law serving our country.

To get off my pills. Shannon

I pray that all children in our school are successful and that they see themselves as successful.

A job that is spiritually right and financially supportive. Thank you. Jeannie

I want strength to free myself.

Heal my cancer. Rachael

Please pray for the Marlie family. They lost their son Lonny in a tragic car accident this past week. God bless and thank you. Ardel

Help me get over my husband, who left me.

Pray that Lucinda can quit smoking, dear Lord. Amen.

Please grant my money miracle. Elory

I pray for complete health. Mona

Please pray for:
Ben—refrain from drug and alcohol abuse and become closer to God.
Tracey—for help as she receives her sentence.
Kaaron—to have healing.
Thank you.

Please pray for Nicole's and Michael's marriage. They are struggling right now. Thank you

Dear God and Angels, grant us peace and harmony each and every day.

For daughter Julie, who is an atheist—also her husband Rod and children being raised without God. Thank you and God bless.

Pray for peace for all people.

That my biopsy will be benign. A.C.

I pray that I find my place in the world and a man to treat me well.

Help Luanne to be okay and help everyone not to be so sad when she dies.

Please pray and watch over my son Norman. He needs a special angel! His mom and dad and brothers love him very much!

I pray that my grief will diminish and the joy Barry brought to my life will replace it. Lucille

For me to have a child that is healthy and survives this time. Thank you.

I pray that Larry will find peace in Jesus' friendship...and marry me!

I request guidance and direction—where should I live, what shall I do for money? I am open and will to serve the Divine Design of my life. Louise

For Lori's heart to open to God.

A prayer for my daughter, Alisha Ann, for her to not use drugs.

Bless my husband's health—Richard, the love of my life.

To find spirituality in our lives.

Thank you for all abundance for me in every aspect of my life: personally, professionally, financially, emotionally, psychologically. Thank you. Lisa

Please let my baby be healthy when it arrives.

I ask and pray for health, wealth and happiness. Thank you for answered prayers.

Ronald has cancerous tumor on his heart and needs peace of mind, body and spirit.

Please pray for my son and his girlfriend at West Point Academy. God Bless. Rhoda

Please pray for March 27th court date, for mercy from the judge, and God's will be done.

To help me and my wife and son to be stable. Thank you.

That Monica has a speedy recovery from chemotherapy for breast cancer. Thank you.

For healing in our family, for protection of our troops in Iraq and around the world, for peace among nations.

Pray for my mother, that she finds inner peace and truly learns to love herself. G.W.

A safe journey home to Maryland Tuesday. Kathryn

I pray that everyone in my family and all my friends will be happy, healthy, prosperous and safe now and forever. Thank you, Hilary

I hope this store goes far with the angels' wings. God is listening to your prayers. Listen to him. He will tell you the way to go.

Children's Prayers

Dear Lord, I pray that all my family lives long and everyone has great dreams. Amen. Love, Amy

Let us get money to move to Europe and move all our stuff and heal us and get me braces.

Please tell my dead grandmother that I love her and that I miss her a lot.

Please let dad be okay.

Dear angels, I wish the war will be over soon. Protect all our soldiers. Bless them. Bless all my family and friends. Love, Sara

Please make sure my whole family is safe and healthy wherever we go, and please forgive me for all of my sins. Thank you, God. Love, Patricia

I hope that my Grandma gets better from her cancer and lives a long time. Chyenne

Please help my dad not to get sick.

I want a dog farm.

I pray that my family will stay healthy and stay as nice as they are.

I Luve You, Brittany

And finally, left untouched, as perfection can only be:

I Jazmin hope that god and the angles will- pretect the world and pretect my family ana friends. the world. God bless

Those who have pierced the veil
know more intimately the light beyond.

Resources

For information on volunteer organizations or charities within your community, the yellow pages is one of your best guides. You may find yourself being drawn to help out in a special way in your area by volunteering or donating to a specific charity or organization, such as a women's shelter, men's shelter or children's home. Whatever is calling to your heart for your services is what the doctor ordered just for you.

Here are the websites, addresses and phone numbers for some of the organizations that have touched my heart in a profound way:

Childhelp USA
Cofounders: Sara O'Meara and Yvonne Fedderson
www.childhelpusa.org
1-800-4-A-CHILD (1-800-422-4453) hotline
15757 N. 78th St.
Scottsdale, AZ 85260
(480) 922-8212
(480) 922-7061 fax

National Hospice and Palliative Care Organization (NHPCO)
www.nhpco.org
1-800-658-8898
1700 Diagonal Road, Suite 625
Alexandria, VA 22314
(703) 837-1500
(703) 837-1233 fax

Mishka Productions
www.mishkaproductions.com
(480) 970-8543

al-anon
www.al-anon.alateen.org
(888) 4al-anon

Dr. Wayne Dyer
www.DrWayneDyer.com

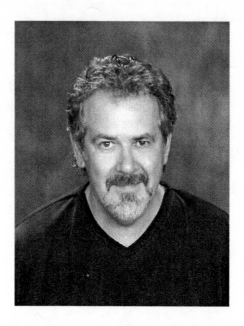

Gerald (Jerry) Van Slyke is an Angel Therapy Practitioner (ATP) and a writer currently residing in Scottsdale Arizona with his wife Pamela. He is working on a series of fantasy/fiction novels and focusing on helping abused children.

www.AngelWingsonFifth.com
moisyhaden@yahoo.com